PRAISE FOR
Secrets of Tracing Your Ancestors

"W. Daniel Quillen's *Secrets of Tracing Your Ancestors* shows those new to the hobby how to begin their genealogy, while showing seasoned family historians some new tricks. Covering the basics such as organization, the best genealogical websites and how to do family group sheets, Quillen approaches his subject with passion and a touch of humor. The book also looks at features of advanced genealogy such as using professionals and writing your personal history. Most chapters feature additional resources pointing readers toward other resources." – *Family Chronicle magazine*

"Your book *Secrets of Tracing your Ancestors* has been extremely helpful to me in a renewal of my genealogy interests." – *Nancy Dailey*

"I would like to thank you for writing a very informative book. There was a lot of information that I did not know about..." – *Donna Perryman Moon*

"I purchased your book and have found it most helpful." – *Glenda Laney*

"Thanks for your help and for writing your excellent book!" – *Laura Johnson*

"I have enjoyed reading your book and I've found excellent leads for finding ancestors." – *Donna Mann*

"... It is not only informative but entertaining. Incorporating your own experiences in brought the book to life. Again, thank you for helping me to understand the many aspects of genealogy and for supplying a roadmap to finding more information about our ancestors." – *Dana L. Hager*

"Of all the books I have looked at yours is the best...and you write with your heart and soul. Thanks for writing such a great book." – *Karen Dredge*

"I got this book out of the library, but before I was half-way through it, I decided I had to have my own copy. Lots of helpful suggestions! I'd recommend it for all new and experienced family historians." – *Margaret Combs*

About the Author

For the past twenty years, W. Daniel Quillen has been a professional writer specializing in travel and technical subjects. He has taught beginning genealogy courses to university students and working adults, and is a frequent lecturer in beginning and intermediate genealogy classes in Colorado. He has compiled his years of genealogical training and research into *Secrets of Tracing Your Ancestors*. He lives in Centennial, Colorado with his wife and children. If you would like to contact him about anything in this book, his e-mail address is: danielmcq@juno.com.

SECRETS OF TRACING YOUR ANCESTORS

W. Daniel Quillen

Cold Spring Press

COLD SPRING PRESS

P.O. Box 284
Cold Spring Harbor, NY 11724
E-mail: Jopenroad@aol.com

This book is dedicated to my grandparents, as well as to all those whose life's passion is discovering their roots.

PHOTO CREDITS
Front cover photo and lower back cover photo: Gilles Dubois from flickr.com. Top two back cover photos: freeparking from flickr.com. Back cover photo, third from top: W. Daniel Quillen.

TABLE OF CONTENTS

Sidebars, Charts & Logs

Remember me in the family tree –
My name, my days, my strife;
Then I'll ride upon the wings of time
And live an endless life.

(Copyright 1996, Linda Goetsch, reproduced with permission)

1. INTRODUCTION

It's like going home to a place you've never been before, or like meeting family for the first time and having a feeling you've always known them.

Genealogy. Family History. **Tracing your Ancestors**. By any name it is one of the most exciting, challenging, fun, insightful, delicious and intriguing things you will ever do. It can become more than a hobby – it can become a passion and an obsession (but the good kind!).

Not only is genealogy considered the number 1 hobby in America, some experts believe it is the number 1 hobby in the world. But why? Why has this seemingly sedentary hobby overtaken the scintillating pastime known as philatelia (stamp collecting)?

Perhaps it is in our very DNA. In the Judeo-Christian tradtion, our first parents (Adam and Eve) kept a genealogy, as did their descendants: the Bible is rife with genealogies from the Old Testament to the New Testament (remember all those "begats?"). In this vein, family bibles often contain rich genealogical information for those individuals lucky enough to have them in their possession.

During America's bicentennial year, Alex Haley wrote and published a book called *Roots*. It was a history of his family from southern slavery to his ancestor's early life in a remote West African village. The ABC network made it into an epic twelve-hour mini-series. About 1.6 million Americans tuned in, and over the eight days that *Roots* was on TV, the genealogical flame in America flared high. As a result of Alex Haley's search for his ancestors, many of us were inspired to search out our own roots. Today, that genealogical flame continues to burn in the hearts and souls of many Americans.

Genealogy is a hobby that can consume you. You'll find it as addictive as eating potato chips and as satisfying as watching a lovely sunset at the end of a hard day's work. There will be times when you will spend many hours, then other times when you put it down for a bit. But like a good friend (or family member!), you can easily pick up where you left off.

Through the pages of this guide, **I'll show you the professional genealogist's secrets**. You'll learn how to begin researching your ancestors. I'll tell you the errors I made in doing research so that you can avoid them. I have provided easy-to-follow instructions and no-nonsense counsel on how to begin, proceed and succeed in this great endeavor. I'll introduce you to more than a few common genealogical hurdles, along with suggestions on how to overcome them.

The **Internet** has touched almost all areas of our society, and it has proven to be a huge boon to genealogists. As you read, you'll learn how to get the most out of the Internet for researching your family history. Throughout the book I show samples of forms that may be of use to you. If you e-mail me at the address listed in the front of this book, I will be happy to e-mail you any of the forms you find in the book. I'll even be happy to provide any guidance I can if you run into problems in your research.

I have also provided in-depth advice on researching various ethnic origins, including African-American, Jewish, Irish, Hispanic and Native American roots, as well as general information on succeeding in research for those ethnic groups not covered in-depth here.

So come along and follow me as we meander our way through old censuses, pore over church records, and find new and exciting ways to discover and learn more about your ancestors. I **promise** it will be a trip you're glad you took!

2. WHY GENEALOGY?

Why is genealogy so popular?

Many societies – Asian, Native American, African and others — kept accurate and extensive genealogies that extended back for hundreds, even thousands of years. Many of them were kept in the memories of tribal Elders and passed on in the oral tradition, spiced with stories of heroism and tragedy from the lives of their forbears.

One might even argue (successfully, I think), that the dusty hobby/ livelihood of archaeology is nothing more than an effort to find man's earliest roots – in other words — genealogy!

Nearly since the birth of the United States, Americans have been interested in who they were and where they came from. Scarcely a dozen years after the signing of the Declaration of Independence, the first census of the United States was commissioned by Congress, and censuses have continued unabated every decade since that time. Our Founding Fathers weren't merely interested in counting the people. The earliest US censuses counted families. They listed the names of heads of households, as well as the age ranges of members of the family and their sex. Since that time, the census instrument has been refined to provide us with great detail on the lives of our progenitors – names, age, sex, number of children, occupation, home owner or renter, and the state or country of the individual's parents' birth.

Before you set out on your genealogical journey, let's set one thing straight. The hobby you are involved in is spelled GeneAlogy, not GeneOlogy. That third syllable, however, can be pronounced either like *al* or *awl* – it makes no difference. By if you are going to pick up genealogy as a hobby, let's make sure you spell it correctly!

GENEALOGICAL HUMOR?

Years ago I was in Richmond, Virginia on business. Since many generations of my family lived and died in Virginia, I decided to stay a few extra days after my business trip to sift through the many genealogical records that can be found in the Virginia State Library there. I mentioned to my work associate that I was going to stay in Richmond a few days after my business was completed.

She said, "Oh, do you have family here?"

I replied, "Yes, but they are all dead."

Dead silence followed. My explanation about staying to do some genealogical research seemed to calm her consternation (a bit).

Before we go much further, let me introduce you to my family. As we go through the book, you'll get to know us better, as I will use many of us to illustrate various aspects and methods of genealogical research.

I am William Daniel Quillen, and I am married to the lovely Bonita Blau Quillen. We have six children. My parents are William Edgar Quillen and Versie Lee Lowrance. They had three children.

My grandparents were:
•Helon Edgar Quillen and Vivian Iris Cunningham. They had one child.
•Elzie Lee Lowrance and Alma Hudson. They had three children.

My great grandparents were:
•Edgar Estil Quillen and Theodora Charity McCollough
•William Edward Cunningham and Emma Adelia Sellers
•Thomas Newton Lowrance and Margaret Ann McClure
•Francis Marion Hudson and Margaret Ellen Turpin

My 2nd great grandparents were:
•Jonathan Baldwin Quillen and Sarah Minerva Burke
•William Lindsay McCollough and Lucy Arabella Phillips
•William Huston Cunningham and Amanda Stunkard
•John Thomas Sellers and Celeste Elizabeth Horney
•Jeremiah Hudson and Frances Duvall

My 3rd great grandparents were:
•Charles Franklin Quillen and Susan or Susannah _____

14

WHY GENEALOGY?

•Samuel McCollough and Elizabeth Throckmorton
•Oliver Sayers Phillips and Charity Graham
•Joseph Cunningham and Sarah Rogers
•Matthew Stunkard and Margaret Peoples
•John T. Sellers and Elizabeth Ritchey
•Leonidas Horney and Jane Crawford

As we progress through the book, I'll use some of these individuals to illustrate search techniques, discrepancy resolution, and perhaps most basically, a much better way to list this information!

GENEALOGY AT WORK

There are many advantages to doing genealogy that go beyond collecting the names of ancestors and putting them in a notebook on your shelf. Here are a few I have come up with, but this is by no means an exhaustive list. You can use the information to:

•come up with meaningful (and sometimes different) names for your children;

•determine a health genealogy (do you have a history of specific ailments in your family that you may want to guard against: heart disease, diabetes, alcoholism, cancer, etc?);

•establish membership in patriotic organizations like The Daughters of the American Revolution;

•meet new friends. Genealogists are among the friendliest people you'll ever meet;

•justify an international vacation (research trip!) to the land of your ancestors' nativity;

•get out of the house: prowling through cemeteries, old courthouses and other places of immense interest.

---

3. GET STARTED

As they say, the longest journey begins at home, and your genealogical adventure need not begin anywhere but within your own home. Start with yourself. A key element of genealogy is to provide information about yourself for your posterity. Now, you may not think that you lead a very exciting life, or that no one would ever be interested in learning about you and your life. But before you know it, you'll have children and grandchildren, even great grandchildren, who would be extremely interested in your life.

Gather all the information about your life that you can find. As you begin thinking and looking, you'll be surprised by the amount of information that is available about you. Here are a few to consider:

Birth Certificates
Birth certificates provide a wealth of information, and are considered a primary source in genealogical research. Consider the information that is generally provided on a birth certificate:

•Your birth date and place;
•full names of your father and mother;
•your parents' address;
•often, your parents' birthplaces;
•occasionally, your parents' occupations.

Remember – just because you know all of this doesn't necessarily mean that a grandson who is interested in learning about you 60 years from now will know it too. His father (your son) may remember some details, but a birth certificate will provide a wealth of information – all accurate. It may also provide the thread to further research, as it provides important information about your parents and their birthplaces. The first time you find a birth certificate of a long-deceased relative you'll know what I mean.

It is not necessary to go to a lot of expense to do this – a photocopy will be fine for your genealogical purposes. There is no need to go to the additional time and expense to get a certified copy, unless you want to.

Baptismal or Confirmation Certificates
Church records such as these often contain as much information about you and your parents as a birth certificate does. In addition, it gives your descendants an idea of your religious convictions – or at least those of your parents.

Graduation Diplomas
While not generally a wealth of genealogical information, high school and college graduation diplomas may shed a little light on your education as well as where you lived as a teen and young adult. These kinds of threads, if found for your ancestors during your genealogical research, might lead you to find the spouse of that ancestor, or perhaps even a sibling or two, especially if the reason you went to that educational institution was because your family moved near there.

Newspaper Articles
Does your local newspaper have a column listing recent births? If so, did your mother clip it out of the newspaper when you were born? It will likely include your parents' names and their address. Were you a superb athlete that was mentioned frequently on the sports pages? As interesting as those articles are to you, you can bet they will be for your grandchildren. How about obituaries? I don't suppose you'll cut your own obituary out, but what about those for your parents, grandparents, etc? Obituaries can be very brief, or they can be very detailed and provide extensive genealogical information about this ancestor of yours. On more than one occasion I have found an obituary that provided a piece of the family history puzzle I was working on for a particular ancestor, and that puzzle piece clarified the picture sufficiently for me to find other puzzle pieces. Were you involved in plays? Did a newspaper article feature your one-man/one-woman art show at the local library? Did you win a local piano competition? Or did your prize steer win Best-in-Class at the local 4-H competition? All of these would be of interest to your descendants.

Was there an article in the local newspaper when you went into the service, or when you became engaged? These too would be good to include in your genealogical collection about you.

SECRETS OF TRACING YOUR ANCESTORS

Photographs

All right — confess. You have hundreds, perhaps thousands of family pictures – and not a single one is in a labeled photo album, nor do any of them have a single thing written on the backs of them, much less basic information such as who is pictured and the date of the picture. Don't dismay – you are not alone. This can be a huge project in and of itself. In fact, an entire industry has sprung up around photo albums.

However, it isn't necessary to get real fancy or painstakingly detailed, nor is it necessary to spend hundreds of hours cataloging and mounting photos. I'm suggesting just the basics here. You don't need to write on every picture in all those boxes and closets – just go through that mammoth pile and begin gleaning photos from various stages of your life – infancy, childhood, adolescence, young adulthood, early marriage, etc. If you have just one or two photos (or three or four) from each period of your life that would be a wonderful start. Write on the backs of these photos as much information as you can remember.

If you can't remember what year a photo was taken, just approximate: "Dad and me at Lake Isabel in southern Colorado when I was 12 or 13 – about 1968 or 1969." Some information will be far better than none.

PRECIOUS HISTORY DISCOVERED

In my role as family genealogist, I pestered my grandmother for years for information about her family. She shared a few small photos of her parents when they were in their 80s. After my grandmother's death, my parents went to Oklahoma to help my grandfather pack up the house so that he could move in with them in their home in Colorado.

While going through their personal effects of nearly 60 years of marriage, my parents discovered a box in the corner of their old Model T garage that contained perhaps 400 photographs in it. Each picture had been meticulously labeled by my great grandmother with the date the photo was taken and the names of all individuals in the photo.

The photos were of several lines of our family, and I was able to match the information on the photos with the genealogy this great grandmother had written in the center section of the family Bible. It was a remarkable find, a precious discovery.

Government Documents

Sometimes we have experiences in our lives that go on permanent file with the government, and for a small fee you can get copies of documents. Included here are military papers and marriage or divorce records.

Memorabilia

Did you keep the tickets from the Dodgers game your dad took you to when you were 6 years old when you were on vacation in Los Angeles? How about those tickets to the Broadway play *The King and I* when you and your sweetheart were first married? While they may have faded with age, you can be assured they will be of great interest to your descendants some day. So gather all that information out of the shoe boxes on the top shelf of your closet, or the top right-hand drawer of your dresser, etc.

Some documents that fall into the Memorabilia category are those associated with your family: the program from a funeral for a grandparent, the program from your child's baptism and so on. Be sure to include these in your collection as they will provide information about you and those you loved to those who follow.

Miscellaneous

This list isn't exhaustive – I have just provided a few of the more obvious items with which to begin your genealogical collection. If you run across other items during your genealogical foraging that you think will be of interest to your posterity, by all means keep it.

Now that you have gathered all this information for yourself, expand the search to each and every member of your household. Do it for your spouse and children – no one in your current household should be immune from your quest!

Shifting Gears

Up to this point, you have been gathering what I call physical genealogical evidence – birth certificates, diplomas, church and government records, etc. Now it is time to shift gears and begin gathering genealogical *information* – the intangible information that you need to help you identify your ancestors. And the best place to start? With yourself.

Yes – that's right – begin with yourself again. You may be surprised by how much you already know, especially about those relatives that are closest to you – your siblings, parents and grandparents. Start with each person, and write down everything you know: full name, nicknames, date of birth, birthplace, places lived, etc. Unless you are absolutely certain,

SECRETS OF TRACING YOUR ANCESTORS

I would check the information with each person after you have written it down. A personal visit, phone call, e-mail or letter are all appropriate, depending on your individual circumstances.

Once you have captured everything you know, it is time to work with members of your extended family to find out what knowledge they have about the family. This is a valuable way to spend your time, especially since many of these family members may be aging and once they leave this earthly existence their knowledge will go with them.

Most genealogy guides suggest beginning with your parents. I suppose I will support that suggestion, although I will do so with one *caveat*. Almost every family I know of has someone – generally an older relative – who is considered the family genealogist, or if not the family genealogist, the one person in the family who just seems to have an interest in and who remembers all the pertinent facts about the family. In my case, it is my Great Aunt Ruth, my grandfather's sister. Of all my extended relatives, she seems to be the one who has the most interest in and knowledge of the history of the family.

If you have an "Aunt Ruth" in your family, then I would suggest starting with her. If she lives in town or nearby, then arrange to meet her to talk about the family. If it is not practical because of distances, then the telephone is a wonderful genealogical instrument. E-mail is a possibility, but I find most of the people from my grandfather's generation are not computer literate. Finally, the postal service is another possibility.

Okay, so you have settled on your family's Aunt Ruth to begin with. What do you do? Where do you begin? Well, first, you need a plan. What are you going to ask? What information is most necessary for you to find out, and what information is she likely to be able to supply? Here are some questions you might consider asking her:

•What was your father's full name? Did he use any nicknames?
•Where was he born?
•When was he born (at least the year)?
•Did he ever leave his hometown? If so, where did he go, and why?
•What did he do for a living?
•Was he ever in the military?
•What were his parents' names? Where were they from? Do you
    remember his mother's maiden name?
•Did he have any siblings? How many? Was he the oldest, youngest, in
    the middle?

GET STARTED

•Do you know the names of his siblings? How about their ages? (Was Aunt Susie two years younger than your dad?)
•What did he look like? Do you have any pictures of him? Who would have some if you don't?

And don't forget these kinds of questions:

•What are your favorite recollections of him?
•Did he have a sense of humor? Or a hot temper (that runs in my family!)?
•Did he love animals?
•What did he do for fun and relaxation?
•What do you miss most about him?
•What are some of your favorite stories from his life?

After you finish getting information about her father (your great grandfather), ask those same questions about her mother, her brothers and sisters, her aunts and uncles, etc. It may not be possible to get all the genealogical information you would like in one visit, so plan to come again.

As you glean information from older relatives, be sure and try to get more than just facts and figures. See if they remember any stories about their parents or grandparents that they can share. Did great grandpa have some hair-raising war stories? Any close calls faced by family members through the years? Ask questions about their health - especially what their cause of death was. Information like this may provide you with important health information for yourself. You'll learn whether there is a history of diabetes / heart disease / stroke, etc., that might be very good for you to know. If several generations of the men in your family died of heart attacks in their 50s, it would be a good thing for you to know and attend to.

When interviewing, pretend you are in school. Date your paper. Put your name on it. Write down who you are interviewing. You may think you'll always remember those things, but after a few years the specifics will fade, I guarantee you.

My editor once gave me the key to being a successful travel guide writer, and I think it applies to genealogists too, especially as it relates to interviewing relatives. He said, "You must be curious. Don't just get the facts, get the facts behind the facts." So - be curious.

SECRETS OF TRACING YOUR ANCESTORS

Be sure and ask for maiden names, nicknames and pet names. My great grandmother was named Theodora Charity McCollough, but everyone called her Dolly. And her mother was always called Grandma Mac.

Caution!
One caution here – don't make this feel like an inquisition. Make it a pleasant experience. If your Aunt Ruth is comfortable with it, bring a video camera and set it off to the side (so she can hopefully forget it is even there), and just let her talk. If a video camera isn't a possibility, then try a tape recorder. Again, if she is more comfortable try keeping it out of sight so as not to intimidate her. Ideally, you can glean the information by just having her talk about her daddy. Occasionally you might supply a question or two (from the list above or others that occur to you throughout the course of the conversation) that will redirect the conversation. But don't be in a rush to get the information and get out the door – this has the potential of being a great time for both of you. You get to learn first-hand information about one of your ancestors, and your Aunt Ruth gets to reminisce about her dad – a win-win situation for all parties concerned.

During the course of your visit, determine whether she has any documents that might further your quest for information. Often, as one of the few in the family who are interested, birth certificates, death certificates, marriage certificates, etc., find their way to the Aunt Ruth in each family. Ask to see them, and come prepared to copy information from them. If there is time and an opportunity, you may wish to see if she will allow you to photocopy the documents.

A 35mm camera is good for taking photographs of photographs that your Aunt Ruth may have. I have several photos of ancestors that look nearly as good as the originals themselves. For best results, use muted natural light. This can be accomplished on a day that is slightly overcast, or under a shaded patio during a sunny day. You can use the same camera for taking pictures of various documents if a photocopier isn't available. Another word of caution here: Be careful – don't take as Gospel the memories of your relatives, even the Aunt Ruth of your family. Sometimes you can end up on a wild goose chase. For example, one relative thought my great grandmother was born in Arkansas. I spent a great deal of time searching Arkansas for her and her family with no luck. Then, when I mentioned my dead-ends to another relative, she responded with, "Well, that's because she wasn't born in Arkansas - she was born in Texas. She was embarrassed that she was born there, so she told everyone she was born in Arkansas." So – recognize this information for what it often is: the best knowledge available at the time. It can lead you to real treasures, or it can lead you down the wrong paths.

Finally, be persistent. I had been searching for the birth information for a great aunt of mine. Family tradition held that she was born in Cottonwood Falls, Kansas. A search of vital records there turned up her three brothers, but not her. One time when I was fresh off another disappointing dead end on this great aunt, I was visiting my folks while on a business trip. While I was there, my grandfather's three sisters and a cousin dropped in for a visit. I once again asked my Aunt Ruth about Aunt Agnes, and she once again confirmed her understanding that Agnes was born in Cottonwood Falls, Kansas. At that point, the cousin (who I had never before met, nor have I seen since) piped in and said that No, Agnes hadn't been born in Cottonwood Falls, and that the family moved there when she was a little girl. She thought they had lived in Sharon Springs before moving to Cottonwood Falls. A search of the county birth records for Sharon Springs confirmed it as my Aunt Agnes' birthplace.

For the record, these kinds of coincidences *happen all the time* for genealogists. When my great aunts and their cousin dropped by for a visit with my folks, I just happened to have been there from my home in New Jersey and my aunts had driven up from Oklahoma to my parents' Denver home.

Other Records
When you are visiting older relatives (including your parents!), they often have information-oozing genealogical records around their house in old trunks, in attics or in the rafters of the old garage. Here are a few items that often provide genealogical information:

Old Letters
If you can lay your hands on old family letters, they can shed a great deal of light on your family. They provide a peek into their lives. And they often contain information about the family that either confirms information you already have, or that sends you off on a search to confirm information contained therein. A letter written by your great grandmother to her "Dearest Sister Sadie," can be a great clue, especially if you never knew that she had a sister named Sadie!

Years ago I found a letter my great grandmother wrote to her brother. She had spent time with their sister during the last week of that sister's life. The sister was dying of diabetes-related health problems, and my great grandmother was briefing her brother on many aspects of the family. From the letter, I learned:

- •her sister's name
- •her brother's name
- •her sister's husband's name
- •the names of all of her sister's children
- •the date of her sister's death
- •the place of her sister's death
- •that her sister's parents lived in the same town where she lived.

In addition to these important facts, I got a peek into my great grandmother's heart and soul. I felt the pain she must have felt as she described her sister's suffering. I felt the great love she had for this sister and for her sister's family.

Do you have any old family letters? Do any of your older relatives? It may surprise you to learn that there are indeed these kinds of pages of your family's history in existence in old trunks, attics, boxes in the rafters of old garages, etc. Remember, several generations ago letters were the only contact family members often had with one another, and letters were filed away as treasures to be visited many times.

Old Budgets/Ledgers
One of my favorite genealogical finds was a budget my mother wrote down when she and my father were first married. It provided a fascinating peek into their lives at that time, and was probably a fair representation of the American working class at that time in our nation's history. Entries included such things as rent ($55), groceries ($10), utility bills ($12), gas ($10). Of course, this was at a time when my father made $48 per week as a telephone lineman.

Is there something similar in your family? Entries might include information about an ancestor's business or investing decisions. It might include loans to children, siblings or parents (or from any of those sources).

Family Bibles
Well, if your family kept an old family Bible, you are lucky indeed. My great grandmother completed numerous generations of genealogy in the center section of her old family Bible, and it is one of my most precious possessions.

GENEALOGY TERMS

Since you are going to be learning about genealogy, it only makes sense for you to learn the language. Following are some terms that you will want to know and understand (for a more complete glossary, see Appendix A):

Family Group Sheet – this is a document that groups a family together under their father. Included will be a man, his wife and all of his children, along with important information about each person, such as their birth, marriage and death dates and places. It is one of the main forms used in genealogy research.

Family History Center – genealogy libraries staffed by volunteers of the LDS Church where genealogists can access the LDS Church's vast genealogical records. They are open to any genealogist, regardless of religious persuasion.

GED.COM – a standard software format that most genealogy software uses as a standard. If you are using a genealogy program that uses GED.COM, you will be able to share your information with others more easily.

Maternal – used to describe which line of the family tree you are referring to. Your maternal grandfather is your mother's father.

Paternal – used to describe which line of the family tree you are referring to. Your paternal grandfather is your father's father.

Pedigree Chart – this is a chart the will show at a glance what your "family tree" looks like, by showing in graphic form who your parents, grandparents, great grandparents, etc., are. A limited amount of genealogical information is included. This too is an important genealogical form.

Primary Source – these are genealogy records created at the time of the event. A birth certificate would be considered an original record.

Secondary Source – genealogy records where information is provided much later than the event. A tombstone or death certificate would be considered a primary source for death information, but a secondary source for birth information, since it is likely that the birth information was provided many years after the person's birth occurred.

Vital Records – this is the term used to documents that contain information about an individual's birth, marriage and death.

But let me provide this warning about the information you find in family Bibles - it should be considered a secondary source. Unless you know for sure that all the names, dates and places contained in the Bible were written at the time they occurred, you must consider them as secondary sources. Good sources, but secondary nonetheless. The information there will provide a great starting point for additional research.

Photos
Some of my most prized possessions are old photos of my family, and they can yield a wealth of genealogical information, especially if whoever owned them took the time to write on the backs of the pictures. Family photos tipped me off to sons and daughters that I hadn't known existed before I had the picture.

Old photos can also provide clues to help you in your research. Many of the photos I have include the name of the photo gallery they were taken at, and the town of the gallery. While that isn't a guarantee that the family lived there (perhaps they were in town visiting a relative or attending the County Fair), it will likely at least let you know that they lived nearby. An old multi-generation photo that has the date written on the back might indicate that your 2nd great grandfather was still alive at the time the photo was taken, but that a similar family picture taken two years later is missing him, but includes his wife. That gives you a two-year window in which to look for your 2nd great grandfather's death date.

On a personal note, I like to study the fashions in the photos - the clothes, hairdos, brooches, necklaces, pocket watches, etc. I especially like to see what kind of shoes the individuals were wearing. For example, I noticed that in many of my old family pictures, even though the family was dressed in their Sunday-go-to-meeting clothes, they were often wearing old, worn-out work shoes.

Old Legal Papers
I have learned that many older relatives were pack rats and kept many things - old letters, wills, deeds, etc. These too can provide a wealth of information for beginning (and advanced) genealogists. Whether you find them in the possession of your great Aunt Ruth or on a microfilm somewhere, they often provide clues to follow up on.

A will tells you that at least on the date the will was drawn, the individual was still alive! It may also shed light on the names and ages of children, and the married names of some of the daughters. You'll know where they lived at the time the will was drawn, and may even learn of the location of married children. One entry I recall said something like, "…and to my daughter Emma Adelia Sellers Cunningham of Vinita, Oklahoma, I leave…." Other clues are not so obvious. Wills always needed two witnesses, and those witnesses were often members of the family. I have seen wills witnessed by sons-in-law, fathers of sons-in law, brothers and children.

Deeds also provide information about where the family lived, and their relative prosperity at that time in their life. I have been amazed at how many times land changed hands between others, parents and children, in-laws, etc. Of course these relationships aren't always listed on the deeds, but they give us another clue to follow up on. If I found that my great grandfather Jeremiah Hudson had sold some land to a James Dallas Hudson, you'd better believe that I would make a note of that and try to find out just who this James Dallas Hudson was, and what (if any) his relationship was to Jeremiah (and to me).

Family Histories/Genealogies
Sometimes you may run across a family history that has been written - either specifically about your family or about a family that one of your ancestors married in to. They are incredible finds, often containing hundreds if not thousands of names. But remember, the information contained in books such as these should be considered as coming from secondary sources, not primary. In my experience, few of these books, especially those written many years ago, contain any sort of citations indicating where the information came from. From personal experience I can tell you they are great sources of leads, but the information is often erroneous. Be grateful to those who compiled them, but use them wisely.

More Than A Coin Collection
Most genealogists will tell you that genealogy is more than just collecting names. It is learning about each individual and discovering (and appreciating) their role in life and history.

As I research, I often find myself vicariously living the lives of those whom I am researching. I remember spending time with family members in the Virginia State Library. Poring over their vital records there, I found many of my ancestors. I recall vividly my feelings about one particular family. I sorrowed with them as I learned about the scalding death of their oldest child when he was 20 months old. I rejoiced at the birth of his brother sometime later, only to be dismayed at his death only 22 months later. Again, I rejoiced at the birth of another brother but was crushed to learn shortly thereafter of his death when he was 22 months old. My joy at the birth of a fourth son was tempered, fearing the worst for this family. Imagine my joy when I found records that told of his marriage - he had survived childhood.

At the time of this experience, one of my own children was 24 months old. I remember how painful it was to think of losing her at that age, as this family had lost their precious little ones time after time after time. I wept with them, and then wept again. Finally I wept tears of joy. I remember thinking how nervous the parents must have been as they approached this last son's 18-month birthday, then his 20-month birthday, and finally his 24-month birthday. I could imagine the figurative sigh of relief and the lessening anxiety as this son put distance between himself and his 2nd birthday and grew to manhood.

I used to teach genealogy classes to university students. In my first class, I would bring in a page torn randomly from the local white pages. I tried to impress upon them the fact that with this random act, I could learn more about total strangers than they probably knew about their own great grandparents. In addition to knowing the strangers' addresses and telephone numbers, I could also discover their profession, such as real estate agent, attorney, doctor, etc. I could often tell if they had children, and the approximate age of at least one of those children (through the "teen line" white pages entry). On more than a few, I could even tell whether they were married - and I knew their spouse's name.

How about you? Can you pass that test? Do you learn more about total strangers than the ancestors who contributed your red hair or analytical mind?

Getting Started Checklist
___ What do you already know? Write it down!

___ Gather all the materials you already have – birth, marriage and death certificates, miscellaneous memorabilia, etc.

___ Identify relatives that might know genealogical information about the family.

___ Arrange to interview family members who may be able to share information about the family.

___ Be prepared during interviews: audio or video recorder, paper, pencil, etc.

GET STARTED

___ Keep good notes of all research you do, including date, source, place of research, etc.

___ Get copies of government documents, photos, etc.

Additional Resources

Curtiss, Richard D., Gary L. Shumway, Sharon Stephenson, *A Guide for Oral History Programs,* California State University, Fullerton (June 1973).

Mills, Elizabeth Shown, *Evidence!: Citation & Analysis for the Family Historian,* Genealogical Publishing Company (January 2000).

Schull, Wilma Sadler, *Photographing Your Heritage,* Ancestry Publishing (April 1988).

Wright, Norman Edgar, *Preserving Your American Heritage: A Guide to Family and Local History,* Brigham Young University Press (June 1981).

4. GET ORGANIZED

Before you get too far in your genealogical quest, it is wise to develop some way to organize your genealogy. When you are first beginning, your organization will probably be like mine was – very simple. But it will amaze you (it did me!) just how quickly you will amass volumes of papers, notes, photos, documents, etc. A good system of organization will help you keep it all straight and enable you to find information whenever you need to. In the last chapter, we talked about collecting various and sundry genealogical documents: birth, baptismal, marriage and death certificates, awards, etc. Once you have collected them, you'll want a way to keep them safe and a way to find them easily.

There are two kinds of organization: for information you have found, and for information you are searching for. Here are the basics of both:

Information You Have Found
I suggest setting up a simple filing system as you get started. If you keep it simple and do it right, you can expand it as you go, keeping the same basic organizational foundations. I tried several kinds of systems when I began my research, and this one worked best for me. Here are the materials you'll need:

•File cabinet or file box
•Tabbed manila folders
•Three-ring notebook
•Hanging folders
•Tabs for the hanging folders

If you cannot afford or do not have enough room for a filing cabinet, you can get file boxes at your local K-Mart, WalMart or Target pretty inexpensively, and they serve the same purpose. The hanging file folders are an important part of your organization, whether you use a file cabinet or file box.

GET ORGANIZED

Begin by writing down all the surnames (last names) of the families you know you will be doing research for. Initially, this will be a small number, but will grow more rapidly than you will believe. Always use the maiden names of the women in your family tree. Start with all the surnames you are familiar with: your surname, your spouse's, your father's and mother's surnames, your grandparents' surnames, etc. After you have identified these names, put one surname on a small slip of tag-board that will fit into the tabs for each hanging folder. After you have completed each surname, slide it into a clear tab, and then attach it to one of the hanging file folders.

Using the surnames of my family who were "introduced" in the first chapter, I would set up files for the following families:

Burke	Peoples
Crawford	Phillips
Cunningham	Quillen
Graham	Ritchey
Duvall	Rogers
Horney	Sellers
Hudson	Stunkard
Lowrance	Throckmorton
McClure	Turpin
McCollough	

Now take the manila folders and on the small protruding tab, write the following labels:

•Birth
•Correspondence
•Death
•Marriage
•Other records
•Photographs

Each of these files will hold information that is important for the surname you are researching. Place a set of these manila folders in each hanging file folder.

Birth, Death and Marriage Records
This is the place where you will store all records that you come across that provide birth, death or marriage information for the surname you are researching. Initially, it is not important to separate various generations

SECRETS OF TRACING YOUR ANCESTORS

or families. As I work on the Hudson family, for example, I will file all the birth certificates I find for Hudson family members in this one manila folder, which will be contained in the "Hudson" file.

I would include here any birth, death or marriage records you receive, governmental or otherwise. Official birth, death and marriage certificates go here, of course, but I would also include copies of the center section of a family Bible, a handwritten note for the file that indicated Aunt Ruth said Uncle Creed was born on such-and-such a date, etc. With the inexpensive cost of photocopying these days, I would also include the copy of a death certificate in the birth folder if it listed a birth date on it, even though the death certificate also will be in the manila folder marked *Death* in the file. As the file gets full, I might consolidate this kind of duplicate information, but while starting out I would include it.

Since you will be keeping multiple generations of records here, I would file them alphabetically by first name (since all the records in this file will have the same last name).

Correspondence
Although research on the Internet has significantly cut down the amount of correspondence I have, I still have enough to justify a manila folder for correspondence. Here I keep copies of letters and e-mails I have sent out, and responses that I receive.

When you receive a response to an inquiry you have sent – whether full of information or indicating that nothing was found for the particular request – always attach the response to the inquiry. I can tell you from personal experience how frustrating it is months or years later to find a response in a pile of papers, and not know where it came from or what information was originally requested.

Other Records
Include here the other miscellaneous and sundry records that you discover that are of genealogical significance. Copies of wills, deeds, land records, military records, etc. are examples of records that might go in this file. If you find that you are collecting a lot of wills, then by all means start another manila folder titled *Wills*. But until you receive a sufficient volume of wills to justify that, I would use the *Other Records* file for them.

Photographs
Not all of the photographs I have end up in albums, although more than a few do. These might be photos of your great grandfather's hometown,

or the old homestead. They may also be photos of tombstones and other interesting tidbits of genealogical interest. They may also be old family photos your mother or grandmother has reluctantly parted with.

Information for Which You Are Searching

Now let's discuss organization as it relates to information you are searching for. Let me share one of the biggest mistakes I made when I first began doing genealogy. Had I been able to avoid this mistake, I would have saved myself countless hours of research that covered ground I had already scoured. I hope you learn from my mistake, and don't make it yourself.

Remember these three words: *Write it down!* When you are doing research, write down the sources you are searching. Write down the date you made your search. It doesn't really matter where you write it down, just put it down somewhere!

Write it down — no matter what the source, write it down. At the time of your research, you'll think that you'll always remember where you got your information, but that may well not be the case five months (or five years!) from now. And if you end up with conflicting dates or places, it will be important to know (and have documented!) whether the source was Aunt Ruth's memory or the birth certificate in someone else's possession.

Forms

Purchasing or creating forms are some of the easiest ways of keeping you on track when you are researching. First of all, spaces on the forms remind you to look for specific information. They help keep you organized in your research. Also, a good form will give you loads of genealogical information at a glance.

You may purchase genealogical forms in a variety of places. The **Church of Jesus Christ of Latter-day Saints** is one of the premier genealogical organizations in the world, and they have well-designed forms available on their website (www.familysearch.org) or from their Distribution Center in Salt Lake City, Utah (Tel. 800/537-5950). See Chapter 10 for more information on the LDS Church as a resource for genealogy work. The **National Genealogical Society** also has a variety of forms available, and these are also pretty inexpensive. Their mailing address is 4527 17th Street, Arlington, Virginia 22207-2363.

In the pages ahead are a few forms that will assist you in your research.

Research Log

The Research Log will help you keep track of the sources you have searched while looking for information on one of your ancestors. It is a simple form designed to keep you from scouring the same records in search of the same information.

In the example on the next page, I have entered some information dealing with the search for my great grandfather's birth date.

Family Group Sheet

One of the most helpful forms you'll use in your genealogical research is the Family Group Sheet. It will become central to your work, as it helps you group individuals into family groups. Once completed, it provides one-stop shopping for a great deal of family history information.

The top portion of the Family Group Sheet contains spaces for critical information about the husband and wife of the family you are researching. The following information can be collected for each:

•Birth dates and places
•Death dates and places
•Burial dates and places
•Marriage date and place
•Spouse's name
•Name of the father and mother of the husband and wife

Since everyone is someone's child, if you know the father or mother of the husband or wife, you've already got a start on the Family Group Sheet for the next generation. The *Father* from this group sheet becomes the *Husband* on the next Family Group sheet, and the *Husband* on this Family Group sheet becomes one of the children on his father's Group Sheet (got that?!).

After you have completed all the information you have for the husband and wife of this family, below them is the section for the children. You'll have the opportunity to complete basically the same information for them as you did for their parents.

As an example, I have completed the form on pages 38-39 for my second great grandfather's family. As you can see, the form begins with Jonathan Baldwin Quillen and his wife Sarah Minerva Burke. You may note as you scan the information that I have many holes in my research.

RESEARCH LOG

Ancestor's Given Name(s): Edgar Estil **Last name:** Quillen **Page** 1 of __

Research Objective: Find Grandpa Ed's Birthdate. He always said he was born 15 Jan 1880 but the 1880 Census (which was taken June 1, 1880) lists everyone in his family - except him. So I think he may have been born after the census was taken.

Date of Search	Source:	Comments
9 Dec 1998	1880 Lee Co. Virginia Census	All the family but Grandpa Ed are there - Census Date 1 June 1880
3 Aug. 1999	Lee County Virginia Records Book and Gate City, VA.	Grandpa Ed's Birth Info is not recorded, although his brothers and sisters are
6 Aug 1999	Virginia State Library - Vital Statistics Section	I went through 20 years of birth records for Lee Co and there is no record of his birth
7 Jan 2001	FamilySearch.org	Checked records on FamilySearch.org, but there were no records of his birth there

SECRETS OF TRACING YOUR ANCESTORS

Death dates are missing for most of my 2nd great grandfather's children, and I haven't yet found information about most of his children's marriages.

In the top right-hand corner of the form you'll note that this is the first of two pages. That tells you this is a partial listing of my 2nd great grandfather's family – he had nine children, and this form only has room for six of them. The three youngest children are included on another Family Group Sheet.

RESEARCH NOTE ON SURNAMES

Family history is a bit old fashioned (is it redundant to say genealogy is old fashioned?): information about families is found and recorded under the male surname.

Take a look at the front and back pages of the group sheet and familiarize yourself with them. Note that each informational entry has a space to the far right of the line labeled *Source: # X* (where *X* is actually a number). This refers to the line on the back of the Family Group sheet that provides you with the opportunity to cite where the information came from for this particular bit of information. This is a critical aspect of efficient genealogical research; ignore it or be sloppy about it and I promise you will curse yourself later on. Just get into the habit of keeping track of where you got your information and your research will be a lot easier for you.

It is important for you to provide accurate and complete citation information for each bit of data that you have. If more than one source was used for birth date and place information, then each source should be cited. For example, in the case of my 2nd great grandfather, we "know" that he was born in Sullivan, Hawkins County, Tennessee because that is what he told his granddaughter (my great Aunt Ruth). We have estimated his birth date based on the 1870 and 1880 censuses, which list his age as 25 and 35 years old, respectively (1870 – 25 = 1845, and 1880 – 35 = 1845). If we find better sources later (like a birth certificate), we'll change it on the forms.

Note that the dates are listed as day, month (with month listed by the first three letters of the month), and full year. (Using the full year instead of two digit years helps keep ancestors in the right century!) As you do genealogical research, you'll see a variety of formats for dates, but the most common format for genealogists is day, month, and year. Get into the habit of listing dates – at least when doing genealogy – in that

36

manner. If you are not faithful to any particular format, you may find yourself later wondering whether 6/1/1903 is 6 January 1903 or June 1, 1903! 6 Jan 1903 is pretty clear and understandable by you and anyone with whom you share your genealogy.

If you would like an electronic copy of any of these forms, just e-mail me at the e-mail address contained in one of the first few pages of this book, and I will be happy to send you electronic copies of the forms. If you have the electronic versions of the forms, you can put them on your computer and complete them on the computer, using hard copy as your research copies, then transferring the information to the computer.

Alternately, you may purchase forms from a variety of locations and genealogical societies. Most contain basically the same information, but it may be arranged a little differently on each form. Just pick a form that works best for you.

Pedigree Charts
Pedigree charts are line charts that show at a glance an individual's direct ancestors (pedigree charts are sometimes referred to as *Ascendancy Charts*). Beginning at the left-hand side of the chart, you'll find one individual. To his or her right, and a little above and below you'll find his/her parents. Fathers are always listed above the mothers.

In the first chapter of this book, I introduced my family. If you go back to that listing, you'll note that the pedigree chart provides the same information (and more!) in a much more convenient – and informative - format.

As useful as pedigree charts are for seeing a flow of ancestors quickly, they have limited value from a research perspective. First of all, while they do list basic information (birth date and place, death date and place, marriage date and place), they do not list sources for that information. Nor do they list children of the marriage, other than the individual immediately to their left.

Most pedigree charts you come across show four or five generations, and these are best to aid you in your research. Larger, mostly wall-style charts list a dozen or more generations.

If you look on page 40, you'll see a Pedigree Chart beginning with my paternal grandfather.

FAMILY GROUP SHEET

Husband		Page 1 of 2	
Given name(s): Jonathan Baldwin		Last name: Quillen	
Birth date: Abt 1845	Place: Sullivan, Hawkins Co., Tenn.		Source: # 1
Died: 28 Sep 1921	Place: Hartville, Missouri		Source: # 2
Buried:	Place: Hartville, Missouri		Source: # 3
Married: 28 Sep 1870	Place: Jonesville, Lee, Virginia		Source: # 4
Husband's Father: Charles Franklin	Last name: Quillen		
Husband's Mother: Susan or Susannah	Maiden name:		
Wife			
Given name(s): Sarah Minerva	Maiden name: Burke		
Birth date: Abt 1846	Place: Gate City, Lee Co., Virginia		Source: # 5
Died: 22 Sep 1933	Place: Hartville, Missouri		Source: # 6
Buried:	Place: Hartville, Missouri		Source: # 7
Wife's Father's Given name(s):			
Wife's Mother's Given name(s):			
*************Children – List all children in order of their birth*************			
1.	M	Given name(s): Emmett Vance	Last name: Quillen	
Birth date: 12 Dec 1870	Place: Gate City, Lee Co., Va		Source: # 8
Died: 26 Dec 1948	Place:		Source: # 9
Married:	Place:		Source: # 10
Spouse's Given name(s):		Last name:	
2.	M	Given name(s): Thomas Franklin	Last name: Quillen	
Birth date: 18 Jan 1872	Place: Gate City, Lee Co., Va.		Source: # 11
Died: Abt 5 June 1950	Place:		Source: # 12
Married: 7 Jan 1877	Place: Lee Co., Va.		Source: # 13
Spouse Given name(s):		Last name:	
3.	F	Given name(s): Cora Belle	Last name: Quillen	
Birth date: Abt 1874	Place: Gate City, Lee Co. Va.		Source: # 14
Died:	Died:		Source: # 15
Married:	Place:		Source: # 16
Spouse Given name(s):		Last name:	
4.	F	Given name(s): Lizzie Leticia	Last name: Quillen	
Birth date: 3 Apr 1877	Place: Nashville, Davidson, Tenn.		Source: # 17
Died:	Place:		Source: # 18
Married:	Place:		Source: # 19
Spouse Given name(s):		Last name:	
5.	M	Given name(s): William Evan	Last name: Quillen	
Birth date: 15 Oct 1878	Place: Gate City, Lee Co., Va.		Source: # 20
Died: 4 Oct 1869	Place:		Source: # 21
Married:	Place:		Source: # 22
Spouse Given name(s):		Last name:	
6.	M	Given name(s): Edgar Estil	Last name: Quillen	
Birth date: 15 Jan 1881?	Place: Gate City, Lee, Va.		Source: # 23
Died: 6 May 1978	Place: Ralston, OK		Source: # 24
Married: 18 Mar 1904	Place: Ralston, OK		Source: # 25
Spouse Given name(s): Theodora Charity		Last name: McCollough	

FAMILY GROUP SHEET

Source List

#1. Place is from family tradition: from Ruth Wedd, granddaughter. Birth date is estimated from 1870 and 1880 Censuses for Lee Co., Virginia

#2. Family tradition: from Ruth Wedd, granddaughter

#3. Family tradition: from Ruth Wedd, granddaughter

#4. Lee Co. Virginia Marriage Registry, located in Gate City, Virginia. Page 203

#5. Lee Co. Birth Registry, on microfilm at the Virginia State Library in Richmond

#6. Family tradition: from Ruth Wedd, grandaughter

#7. Family tradition: from Ruth Wedd, granddaughter

#8. Record of birth in possession of Daniel Quillen

#9. Record of birth in possession of Daniel Quillen

#10.

#11. Record of birth in possession of Daniel Quillen

#12.

#13. Lee Co. Marriage Registry, on microfilm at the Virginia State Library in Richmond

#14. Family tradition: from Ruth Wedd.

#15.

#16.

#17. Record of Birth in possession of Daniel Quillen

#18.

#19.

#20. Record of Birth in possession of Daniel Quillen

#21.Ruth Wedd

#22.

#23.Personal knowledge (?) of Ed Quillen. Question comes from 1880 Census of Lee Co.

#24. Ruth Wedd

#25. Marriage certificate in possession of Ruth Wedd

Pedigree Chart

Number 1 is the same as number ___ on chart number ___

Chart number ___

8. **Charles FranklinQuillen**
Father of #4
Born: Abt 1826   Place: Stokes Co, NC
Mar: Abt 1844   Place:
Died: Place:

4. **Jonathan Baldwin Quillen**
Father of #2
Born: Abt. 1845   Place: Sullivan Co, TN (?)
Mar: 28 Sep 1870 Place: Jonesville, Lee, VA
Died: 28 Sep 1921 Place:Hartville, MO

9. **Susan or Susannah**
Mother of #4
Born: Place:
Died: Place:

2. **Edgar Estil Quillen**
Father of #1
Born: 15 Jan 1881(?) Place: Lee Co. VA (?)
Mar: 18 Mar 1904   Place: Ralston, OK
Died: 6 May 1978   Place: Fairfax, OK

10. ___
Father of #5
Born: Place:
Mar: Place:
Died: Place:

5. **Sarah Minerva Burke**
Mother of #2
Born: Abt. 1846   Place: Lee Co, VA (?)
Died: 22 Sep 1932/33 Place: Hartville, MO

11. ___
Mother of #5
Born: Place:
Died: Place:

1. **Helon Edgar Quillen**
Born: 18 Jan 1906   Place: Ralston, Pawnee, OK
Mar: 26 May 1928   Place: Ralston, Oklahoma
Died: 6 May 1978   Place: Fairfax, Osage, OK

Spouse of #1 **Vivian Iris Cunningham**

12. **Samuel McCollough**
Father of #6
Born: 10 Feb 1837   Place: of Bristoria, PA
Mar: 3 Mar 1856   Place: Waynesburg, PA
Died: 22 Feb 1871   Place: Waynesburg, PA

6. **William L. McCollough**
Father of #3
Born: 16 Jul 1862   Place: of Bristoria, PA
Mar: 19 Aug 1883   Place: Waynesburg, PA
Died: 9 May 1927   Place: Ralston, OK

13. **Elizabeth Throckmorton**
Mother of #6
Born: 1 Nov 1835   Place: Waynesburg, PA
Died: 25 Dec 1913   Place: Rymer, WVA

3. **Theodora Charity McCollough**
Mother of #1
Born: 22 Sep 1884 Place: Waynesburg, PA
Died: 3 Dec 1971 Place: Fairfax, OK

14. **Oliver Sayers Phillips**
Father of #7
Born: 21 Aug 1829 Place: Prosperity, PA
Mar: 1 Aug 1849   Place: Greene, PA
Died: 17 Mar 1899 Place: Greene, PA

7. **Lucy Arabella Phillips**
Mother of #3
Born: 20 Jun 1860 Place: Waynesburg, PA
Died: 18 Jun 1948 Place: Ralston, OK

15. **Charity Graham**
Mother of #7
Born: 16 Aug 1833 Place: Center Twp., PA
Died: Place:

GET ORGANIZED

Use the three-ring binder I mentioned early in this chapter to store your Family Group sheets, Research Logs and Pedigree charts. Set it up with tabs for each surname you are researching. As you complete each Family Group sheet or pedigree chart, file it under the appropriate tab, and do so sequentially, from one generation to the next. Eventually you may need a notebook for each surname, but to begin with it is okay to combine them all in one notebook.

Get Organized Checklist
___ Gather together all the information you have found – certificates, photos, etc.

___ Decide on an organizational methodology (file cabinet, binders, etc.)

___ Procure materials that will support your method of organization.

___ As you gather information, write it down and then file it!

___ Familiarize yourself with forms that may assist you in organizing the genealogical information you collect.

___ Select the appropriate forms you need to match the information you have.

Additional Resources
Carmack, Sharon Debartolo, *Organizing Your Family History Search: Efficient & Effective Ways to Gather and Protect Your Genealogical Research,* Betterway Publications. (April 1999)

Carmichael, David, *Organizing Archival Records: A Practical Method of Arrangement,* Pennsylvania Historical Society. (February 1993)

Dollarhide, William, *Managing a Genealogical Project,* Genealogical Publishing Company. (May 1999)

Lackey, Richard S., *Cite Your Sources: A Manual for Documenting Family Histories and Genealogical Records,* University Press of Mississippi. (February 1986)

5. WHAT'S IN A NAME?

When I was growing up, one of my classmates was named Eric, and he had copper-colored bright red hair. On one occasion, our sixth grade class was covering a unit on family history and we were each asked to find out about one of our ancestors, and prepare and present an oral report to the class. When the day came for Eric to make his report, he stood in front of the class, blushing to the tips of his ears, and told us that one of his ancestors was Eric the Red, the intrepid Viking explorer....(yeah, right Eric!). As I recall, we had a pretty good laugh at Eric's expense. I never did find out whether he was kidding us or not.

Then again, maybe he wasn't kidding; little did I know then, but through the centuries, many people were named after physical characteristics that they or a relative possessed. In fact, there is a wide variety of naming schemes that might give you a clue to something about your progenitors. Read on for a few thoughts on the topic.

Physical Characteristics
Many of those around us still carry the names of our progenitors that may have once reflected their physical characteristics. Ever know a person whose surname was Klein? Klein means small in German. How about Rubio (Spanish for blonde) or Blanco (Spanish for white)? Delgado means thin in Spanish, and the popular name Rojas may have been once used to identify a strain of the family with red hair (since rojas means red or rosy).

An Animal Connection
Many surnames reflect the names of animals. Perhaps an ancestor handled, raised or sold certain kinds of animals, or perhaps they were just fond of or admired a particular kind of animal. They may have even looked like a particular animal. Consider for example, the following: *Adler* (eagle in German), *Aguilar* (eagle in Spanish), *Haas* (rabbit in German) or *Garcia* (fox in Spanish) or *Fox* (also fox in English). Have you

WHAT'S IN A NAME?

ever known someone named *Leon* (lion in Spanish) or perhaps *Faulkner* (falken is hawk in German)?

Patronymics

Many cultures employed the use of patronymics when taking names for themselves. A patronymic is a name that identifies the named person with his or her father.

The Irish had their own form of patronymics recognized the world over. Prefixes such as Mc or Mac were used to signify the *son of*: McDonnell was therefore the son of Donnell. Another prefix was the O' which meant "descended from," and a grandson or great grandson might use such a prefix. Occasionally the English passed laws to annoy the Irish (actually, they were trying to assimilate them into English culture). One such law forbade the use of the patronymics *O'* and *Mc*. At that time, the patronymic *fitz* replaced *Mc* for son of: Fitzmorris then meant the son of Morris.

Almost as prevalent as Irish patronymics are Scandinavian patronymics. I suppose we all know more than our fair share of individuals with surnames like Anderson (Anders' son) and Johnson (John's son). For centuries Scandinavians employed this naming scheme, and until surnames became common (in the late 1700s or early 1800s depending on the location), the names changed from generation to generation.

The Jewish culture also has its patronymics. You will occasionally see the name *ben* used to designate the son of, as in David *ben* Joseph (David, the son of Joseph). Certain Jewish groups also used patronymics to honor living grandparents, and there was a specific order used to designate names. The first-born son was often named after his paternal grandfather, and his brother (the second son) was named after his maternal grandfather. They used this practice for their daughters too: first-born daughters were given the name of their paternal grandmother and second-born daughters received the names of their maternal grandmother. This method of naming was especially popular with Sephardic Jews.

The French adopted the term fitz to mean son of: Fitzpatrick was therefore the son of Patrick (fitz was derived from the French work fils, which means son).

Spanish surnames are often derived from patronymics. In Spain and Portugal, an abbreviated way to identify a person with his or her father was by the addition of az, ez, iz, or oz to their father's last name. For instance, Julio, el hijo de Rodrigo became Julio Rodriquez (Julio, the son of Rodrigo).

And let's not forget that the Russians also used patronymics. It was common for Russians to have as their middle name the name of their father, with a –*vitch* added for the sons or –*evna or -ovna* added for their daughters. If I may borrow from author Leo Tolstoy's epic novel *Anna Karenina*, I will give you a few examples to illustrate this. The main character in the novel is Anna Arkadyevna Karenina – Anna, the daughter of Arkady. Her brother is Stepan Arkadyevich Oblonsky – Stepan, the son of Arkady. Konstantin Dmitrievitch Levin (Konstantin, son of Dmitri) was enamored with Anna's sister-in-law: Katarina Alexandrovna Oblonsky (Katarina, daughter of Alexandr), and Anna's lover was Alexey Kirillovitch Vronsky (Alexey, the son of Kirill), much to the dismay of her husband, Alexey Alexandrovitch Karenin (Alexey, the son of Alexandr). Phew!

While that may seem overwhelming, your Russian ancestors' very names may well contain clues to their next generation by providing their father's name.

DON'T DO IT!

I can almost guarantee you that at some time or other in your research you will run across information that you'll "know" just isn't right. The temptation will be to correct the information rather than just write down what you have found.

Don't do it!

Perhaps it's the first name of an ancestor. While you might be absolutely certain that your great great grandmother's name is Theodora, if you find her listed in a US Census as "Dolly," that is the name you should record as you copy the data down. Or perhaps it's your last name that has been spelled creatively. Resist the temptation to substitute the information that is different. Copy the record exactly as you find it so that you can have an accurate representation of what you found.

Occupations

I suppose like most Americans, throughout your lifetime you have known many individuals named Miller, Smith, Carpenter, Carver, Schneider,

WHAT'S IN A NAME?

Guerrero and Escobedo. Each of these surnames may be indicative that an ancestor owned or worked at a mill (Miller), was a blacksmith (Smith), built things (Carpenter), was one who carved (Carver), earned his keep as a tailor (Schneider means tailor in German), a soldier (Guerrero means soldier or warrior in Spanish) or worked as a sweeper (Escobedo).

How about names like Joiner (construction term), or Metzger (German for butcher). I've a friend whose mother's maiden name was Kirchebauer – German for church builder. My friend Karl Fischer might be descended from a man who fished for a living (since fisch is the German name for fish). Do you suppose you can figure out the occupation of at least one of the Weaver ancestors?

Geographic Locations
Don't overlook the possibility that your surname is derived from a town, country, or physical geographic attribute associated with an ancestor. I once had two roommates named Mike. We called one Mike Jersey because he was from New Jersey. The concept is the same. Let's say there were two Mikes who lived near the same village several hundred years ago, before surnames were common. One lived by a lake, and the other at the foot of a hill. They might have been called Mike Lake and Mike Hill, respectively. I had a friend named Duane Alleman once, and I'd be willing to bet at least one of his paternal ancestors was German (Alemán is the Spanish word for German) who lived someplace where Spanish was spoken. Or how many people are you acquainted with who have the surname French? I'd wager somewhere in their family tree is a French ancestor.

As you climb your family tree, it is fun to be aware of these things – it just adds another element to your detective work.

Mother's Maiden Names
Another fairly common naming custom has been the use of the mother's maiden name by one or more of her sons. I was once doing research on one of my family lines, and I came across a fellow named Hartle Hart Sellers. I wondered if Hart might not be his mother's maiden name, and sure enough, after much research, I found that Hart was indeed her maiden name. Again, a genealogical clue right in the midst of your ancestor's name!

Don't Assume...
As you are doing your research, don't fall into the trap that I once fell into. As a relatively inexperienced genealogist, I was doing research in

central Pennsylvania. I was scouring the 1880 US Census, and discovered that one of my ancestors had married a young woman by the name of Mahalia. What an interesting – and unique! – name that was. To determine her maiden name, I decided to search the 1870 US Census, when she would have been 11 or 12 years old. I reasoned that if I could find an 11- or 12-year-old girl named Mahalia in one of the families in that county, I would probably have found her maiden name, since Mahalia was such an odd name.

Sure enough, after just a little bit of searching, I found a Mahalia listed with her family not far from my own family on the census. I happily penned her maiden name on my forms and went merrily on my way.
It wasn't until years later when I was doing additional research in that same county that I discovered that contrary to my assumption, Mahalia was a very common name in 1870 Pennsylvania! Further research into other records proved the fallacy of my earlier assumption about her maiden name.

Another example – my brother-in-law had a great-great uncle named Adam. Adam died as a little boy. The next son born to that same family was named Adam after his older brother. He also died. Finally, a third son was born to the same family, and he too was named Adam. This Adam lived, but as my brother-in-law did his research, he had to be careful to get the right birthdate for the right Adam!

Spelling Woes
Here's a hint that is probably heresy to my 6th grade teacher: Don't limit yourself to only one spelling of your name. In my research, in nearly every one of my family lines, at one time or another I have found variations in the spelling – sometimes within the same generation! Here are a few examples from my own family:

•Sellers, Sellars, Sellar
•Ritchie, Ritchey, Richey
•Horney, Harney
•Quillan, Quillen, Quillon, Quillin, McQuillan, McQuillon, etc.
•Lowrance/Lorentz
•McCollough/McCullough
•Rogers/Rodgers
•Throckmorton, Throgmorton
•Hudson/Hutson
•Graham/Grimes

WHAT'S IN A NAME?

And just because you are a Smith or a Jones (by the way - is it true that the surname of Adam and Eve was Jones?), don't assume you are immune from spelling changes: Smith/Smythe/Smithy/Schmidt or Jones/Jonas/ Joans, etc.

There are many reasons for this, and your creative detective work will have to gather all the threads together into one cohesive answer. Immigration officials are often accused of this, but in my opinion that happened far less than was alleged. It may have been an immigration official, or it may have been illiteracy. The spelling of my surname may be an example of the latter. The family tradition is that several generations of my farming ancestors saw no use in sending their children to school. When the first kids in 75 years went to the local one-room schoolhouse, the teacher asked how they spelled their last name (the correct spelling was Quillan). The children responded that they didn't know, so the teacher "taught" them how to spell it: Quillen. No one at home knew better, so the spelling is the one my line of the family uses today. True story or false? I don't know, but I have seen family members' names spelled differently on US Censuses, marriage licenses, birth certificates, and so on.

Another reason might be that a newly immigrated family wanted to fit in to their newly adopted country. In that case, Meier became Meyer, Schneider became Snider, Schmidt became Smith and Blau became Blue. In my family, McQuillan became Quillan.

What's in a Name? Checklist

____ Write down all the possible spellings you can think of for the surname you are researching.

____ Don't ignore surnames that are similar to but spelled differently than the one you are researching.

____ Look for clues in your name that might indicate where an ancestor was born, or might indicate a possible occupational clue.

____ Watch for patronymics and learn how to use them to help you in your ancestral search.

____ If you come across a name that is spelled differently than how you think it should be spelled, write it down exactly as it appears in the research record.

___ Because a name sounds strange or odd to your 21st-century ears, that doesn't mean it wasn't very common in the era or area where you are researching.

___ Watch for middle names that might give a clue to a mother's maiden name.

Additional Resources
Rose, Christine, *Nicknames: Past and Present*, Rose Family Association, 3rd edition. (May 1998)

6. VITAL RECORDS

Vital records are those records that are critical to successful and accurate genealogical research. They are quite frankly the goal every genealogical researcher should strive to achieve for each ancestor they are researching. They are original records that provide information about the names, dates and places of births, marriages and deaths of those for whom you are searching.

These important and original records will often shed a great deal of light on the family you are researching. I have seen birth certificates, for example, that contain some or all of the following information:

•Individual's full name
•Birth date
•Place of birth
•Residence of parents (if different than birthplace)
•Mother's full maiden name
•Mother's age at the time of this birth
•Number of children born previously to this mother
•Father's full name
•Father's age at the time of this birth
•Father's occupation
•State or country of origin of parents

Death certificates likewise contain some of the same information, adding the death date, cause of death and the spouse's name. Marriage certificates often provide just the basics: full names of the bride and groom and the date and place of the marriage. Marriage registers, however, often contain more information about the couple, including parents' names and the age of the bride and groom. Marriage registers were books that were kept by the local government (typically the county) of all marriages occurring within its boundaries.

Where to Look?

So now that you know what vital records are, where do you go to find them? Bear in mind that entire books have been written on this very topic. One of the most exhaustive and a definite resource to obtain to aid you in your research is George B. Everton's *Handy Book for Genealogists: United States of America*. It is a thorough guide that will help you find just about any type of government record available — federal, state, or county. It covers every type of governmental record conceivable and details time periods those records are available in each jurisdiction. Over 600 pages of incredible detail await you. In addition to providing you with what information is available, it also tells you how to go about getting it: where to write and who to address your letter to.

Each state requires the housing of vital records for their state. Some of these states required those records to be centralized for easier access, while others simply required each county or city to keep the records. That is why a good resource book such as George Everton's *Handy Book for Genealogists: United States of America* is invaluable. It will guide you to the right place the first time. Without a resource like that, you will not know whether to write to the State Department of Vital Records or the local county courthouse where your ancestor was born.

Another option for finding where to write if you are computer literate is to search the Internet for the offices of Vital Records (sometimes called Vital Statistics) for the various states. Ancestry.com has a nice feature that is available without subscription. It lists all the states, their mailing addresses and the websites of their Vital Records departments. It also provides lists of records that are available, and the dates those records are available, along with the cost of copies. The Ancestry.com website is www.vitalrec.com.

Another organization that provides similar information is the National Center for Health Statistics, and their website is *www.cdc.gov/nchs/howto/w2w/w2welcom.htm*. In addition, most of the states have a similar website. You may find that website by entering *(State name) Department of Vital Records* in your search engine. Alternately, I have provided the addresses, phone numbers and websites of each state's Department of Records at the end of this book in Appendix C. Each entry also lists the cost of birth and death certificates.

VITAL RECORDS

What Do I Say?

Writing for information need not be a complicated and drawn-out affair – in fact, it should be very simple. But there are a few "rules" that you should follow when writing to request information:

1. Always include a self-addressed, stamped envelope (SASE) with your request. Use a #10 business envelope.

2. Always include your return address underneath your signature (just like you were taught in school). Letters and envelopes often get separated; this will ensure that the clerk handling your request will have your address.

3. Keep your request simple: don't request fourteen bits of information. For example, request one or two marriage certificates at a time, rather than three marriage certificates, two birth certificates, a death certificate and two wills. You will likely find that your total request will be filled more quickly if you break it up into bite-size pieces.

4. Include payment if you know how much it is. If you do not know the cost, then send a query letter prior to your request asking for the costs. (Note: with today's low long-distance rates, I have found it less expensive – and quicker! – to call for this information.) Your payment should be by personal check or money order – never send cash!

5. Be specific about your request – what are you looking for, when did the event occur, and for whom?

6. If the name (first or last) could have been spelled differently, include that different spelling in your request. Otherwise, a clerk may decide that the record he has for Jonathan B. Quillan does not match the request you sent for a birth certificate for Jon Quillen.

7. Include a date range that you are looking for. Generally try to keep the range to five years or less.

8. Include other data that may help the clerk find the right record (parents' names, where you believe the event occurred, cemetery they were buried in, etc.).

SECRETS OF TRACING YOUR ANCESTORS

Here's a sample letter requesting information about my great grandfather:

March 15, 2003
Virginia Office of Vital Records
P.O. 1000
Richmond, VA 23218-1000

Dear Vital Records Department,

I would like to request a photocopy of the birth certificate of my great grandfather, **Edgar Estil Quillen** (may also be spelled Quillan, Quillon, Quillin). I believe he was born in Lee County between 1879 and 1882. His parents were Jonathan Baldwin Quillen and Sarah Minerva Burke. I have enclosed $10.00 for the birth certificate search, as your website indicates that is the cost. I have also enclosed a SASE for your convenience.

Thank you,

Daniel Quillen

Note that the request is short and sweet and to the point. It is for one request, lists several possible spellings of my great grandfather's last name and provides other information that might help the clerk identify the right record (his parents' names, a range of birth years and the county of his birth). I have also enclosed a check for the correct amount for the birth certificate.

What Do the Records Cost?
The costs for obtaining copies of birth, death and marriage certificates vary from state to state. At the time of this writing, prices range from $4.00 to $35.00, which covers the cost of searches as well as copies of certificates that are found. Most states will not issue a refund if a copy is not found, but will send a letter indicating that a search had been conducted with no success.

Friendly Caution
One caution – always try to discover those records of a person's life that were kept nearest to the event. For example, a death certificate might also contain some of the same information as a birth certificate – the person's name, date and place of birth, parents' names, etc. However, that information might have been written down 70 or more years after the event took place, and is likely to be completed by those who were not present at the time. Dimming memories of those who provided the information may have not quite recalled the correct dates or places.

In fact, the information may have been provided by a sibling, cousin or neighbor who never did have quite the exact information. Does that invalidate the information about birth and parentage found in a death certificate? Not necessarily. Just treat it as a clue to assist you in your search for documentation a little closer to the person's birth.

Vital Records Checklist
___ Determine which ancestor you want to get information about.

___ Gather the information you already know about this person (name, place of birth, approximate birth year, etc.)

___ Locate the Vital Records department of the state or county where your ancestor's birth, death or marriage may have taken place. This may be found in Appendix C, on the Internet, or through a book written specifically for this purpose.

___ Write a letter to the state's Vital Records Department, requesting the certificate you are looking for. Make sure to:
    ___ Include a self-addressed, stamped envelope (SASE)
    ___ Include a check or money order (never cash!) for the cost of the certificate.
    ___ Be specific in your request.
    ___ Do not request too many certificates at one time.

Additional Resources
Bentley, Elizabeth Petty, *The Genealogist's Address Book*, Genealogical Publishing Company. (February 1991)

Dollarhide, William, (Alice Eichholz, editor), *Ancestry's Red Book: American State, County and Town Sources,* Ancestry Publishing. (May 1997)

Everton, George B., *Handy Book for Genealogists: United States of America*, Betterway Publications, 9th edition. (September 1999)

Kemp, Thomas Jay, *International Vital Records Handbook*, Genealogical Publishing Company; (August 1994)

Melnyk, Marcia, *Genealogist's Handbook for New England Research*, New England Historic Genealogical Society, 4th edition. (January 1999)

7. GENEALOGICAL SOCIETIES

You would expect that any hobby that has as many participants as genealogy does would have many organizations of like-minded people who get together and share their information and expertise. And so it is with genealogy. Literally thousands of genealogical organizations have sprung up through the years in support of this pastime. One or more of them may be just the answer you are looking for to help you find information on your family. And since some of them have been around in one form or another for as much as 150 years, the information they have gleaned on their family lines is often extensive.

A visit to the Internet confirms the existence of these societies, and their willingness to share their information and expertise. The last time I typed "genealogy society" on **Yahoo!** yielded nearly 700 organizations who have websites dedicated to genealogy. Some are area-specific (e.g., Germany, Hancock County, Maine, San Mateo, etc.) and others are family-specific. Some are societies that just provide information, support and expertise to their members. Another source of information on genealogical societies is the **Federation of Genealogical Societies** located at *www.fgs.org*. It boasts over 500,000 members and over 500 family associations and genealogical societies in its membership. By searching for these societies on the Internet, you can find out about their existence, mail and/or e-mail address, as well any website and telephone numbers that are available.

Membership in most of the genealogical societies is the modest cost of annual dues ($15 to $35 per year). The dues may include access to family or area genealogical information as well as a quarterly newsletter focusing on genealogical aspects of the family or region.

These societies can be of immense assistance to beginning genealogists. Several years ago while doing research for another book, I ran across a list of genealogy societies. Scanning it quickly, I noticed the Hudson

GENEALOGICAL SOCIETIES

Family Association. My grandmother was a Hudson, and despite a number of efforts to learn more about her line, I knew virtually nothing about the family beyond her grandfather. So almost as an afterthought, I jotted down the address, and a few days later I fired off a short letter:

Dear Hudson Family Association,

I came across your organization in *Moore's Book of Lists*. My grandmother is a Hudson, so I would like to join your organization. The entry in the book didn't have much information about your society, but I am enclosing $50 for dues. If that is too much, please send me as many back issues of your newsletter as the extra amount will purchase.

Thank you,

Daniel Quillen

I am by nature an optimist, so I was cautiously optimistic that the Hudson Family Association would be able to assist me in my Hudson ancestral pursuit. I was totally unprepared for the amount and quality of assistance they gave me.

Within days I received a note welcoming me to the Hudson Family Association. They explained that the association was formed to further genealogical research on the family line, and asked whether I would be willing to share information about my side of the family.

I was happy to share the information (genealogists are like that!) and I shared my information, as scanty as it was. I shared birth and marriage information about my current family, my grandmother, her parents and her paternal grandfather's name and place of birth.

A few weeks later, I received my first copy of the *Bulletin Hudsoniana*, the Hudson Family Association newsletter. One section was devoted to welcoming new members. Imagine my unbounded joy when I found the following entry:

Welcome New Members!
Quillen, W. Daniel:
William Daniel Quillen, born 27 Feb 1956, Lynwood, Los Angeles, CA married 13 April 1979 Bonita BLAU; children: William Michael, Katie Scarlet, Joseph Daniel, Andrew Teague, Emily, Jesse Lee Blaine.
Versie Lee LOWRANCE, born McClain, OK, married 13 July 1951 William Edgar Quillen, born Norman, OK;

Alma HUDSON, born 24 Apr 1913, Stephens, OK, married 5 Oct 1932 Elzie Lee LOWRANCE, born 24 Feb 1906, Wayne, OK;

Francis Marion HUDSON, born 13 Nov 1877, Pope, AR, died 12 Jan 1960, Los Angeles, CA, married 1909 Margaret Ellen TURPIN;

Jeremiah HUDSON, born 1851, AR, died 1914, Dibble, OK, married about 1873 Frances DUVALL, AR;

Francis Marion HUDSON, born 20 March 1829, Lauderdale County, AL, married about 1848 Mary ____;

Jeremiah HUDSON, living 1830 in Lauderdale County, AL, married Lavina JONES, living in 1830 in Lauderdale County, AL;

Levi HUDSON, married Hannah ____;

Major HUDSON, born about 1690, died 16 Nov. 1781, Worchester County, MD, married Martha GILLETT;

Henry HUDSON, born 8 July 1669, Somerset County, Maryland, died 24 Dec 1720, Somerset County, MD married (1) ____ LUDLONG?, (2) Ellis DENNIS;

Henry HUDSON, born about 1642, Accomack County, Virginia, died about 1710, Somerset County, Maryland, married about 1664 Lydia SMITH;

Richard HUDSON, born 1605, England, died about 1657, Northampton County, Virginia, married (1) Mary ____, married (2) Mrs. Mary HAYES, married (3) Barbara JACOBS;

William HUDSON, born about 1570, London, England, married about 1603 Alice Turner;

Henry HUDSON born about 1541

They had taken the scant information I had provided them and tied me back in a direct line of ancestors to 1541 – 13 generations and 450 years! A subsequent request from me provided Family Group Sheets on every family member along with documentation of each name and date – hundreds of names and a great deal of vital statistic information. A wonderful find indeed.

I share this story to assure you that no matter how alone you may feel in your research sometimes, there are often many people out there who have already found the very information you are searching for. And the best part about that message is that they are almost always willing to share that information.

You'll note, by the way, that much of the Hudson family information that was provided to me was unknown, especially the further I climbed the family tree. In a number of instances, there are first names only, or missing dates, or at best approximated dates. That's okay – at least I have information to go on that will help me find some of these people later on.

GENEALOGICAL SOCIETIES

Genealogy societies provide a variety of valuable services, including:
- Timely how-to advice on research for the family or in a particular area.
- Share, share, share information (that's how I got all that information on the Hudson line).
- Preserve and make available records (many societies get involved with microfilming and indexing original records for their members).
- Making your ancestors come alive by providing stories from their lives. Some are humorous, some historical, many are tragic. All serve to help you become better acquainted with your ancestors.
- Recommendations for improving your genealogy research through the announcement (or sponsoring) of seminars or the publication of articles.
- Evaluations of hardware and software used for genealogical purposes.

OLLEY OLLEY OXEN FREE!

Searching for your ancestors is often a little like playing hide-and-go-seek with your four- or five-year-old little brother. He loves the game, but doesn't quite get the rules. Giggling or moving, he seems to delight in being found.

And so it is with many of your ancestors – it seems that often they do all they can to be found. As you work (play!) in genealogy, you'll be surprised at how much information will come to you – almost as though by accident. Through the years I have found that the smallest amount of effort on my part often yields immense genealogical success. Anyone who has done much genealogy at all has multiple stories of amazing coincidences that resulted in genealogical progress – chance meetings with other genealogists working on their line, intuitive feelings leading them to information in least-expected places, etc.

Don't get me wrong – there are still those ancestors out there that seem to be extremely good at playing hide-and-go-seek. Unlike the little brother mentioned at the outset of this section, they are experts at hiding and dodging even your best efforts. They will bring out your best detective instincts! In the mean time, keep looking! If all else fails, try calling, "Olley olley oxen free!" to see if they will reveal their hiding places.

Genealogical Societies Checklist

___ Determine which surnames you wish to do research on.

___ Seek out websites and books that cover Genealogical Societies.

___ Be prepared to share what you know about your family.

___ Be persistent.

Additional Resources

Meyer, Mary Keysor, *Meyer's Directory of Genealogical Societies in the USA and Canada,* Libra Publications, 9th edition. (May 1992)

Federation of Genealogical Societies website: *www.fgs.org.*

8. GENEALOGICAL COLLECTIONS IN LIBRARIES

Thank you, Benjamin Franklin! His idea of public libraries has had many benefits for our society – and especially for genealogists. Many libraries have genealogy sections that are just aching to be searched. A few hours in your local library may yield a surprising amount of genealogical information for you. Whether it is your city library, a national archival center or a small county library, you can often find information that has been buried for years, just waiting to be found.

Family History Library
The Family History Library of the Church of Jesus Christ of Latter-day Saints is indisputably the finest genealogy library in the world. It is so valuable as a resource for genealogists that it has its own separate chapter in this book. Between visits to the library in Salt Lake City, its records that are available through the Internet and its extensive lending library network of over 3,700 Family History Centers (branch offices of the Family History Library), its resources are exceptionally available to individuals no matter where they live. Over 750 million names are in their databases, books and microfilms, and they are all available to genealogists regardless of their religious beliefs.

For more details, be sure and spend some time with the chapter in this book that addresses the Family History Library.

State Libraries
Each state has a major state library, usually located in the state capitol (although not always!). Each of these libraries has a Genealogy section for you to go and search for your ancestors. Depending on the funding the library receives (and has received through the years), their collection may be extensive or somewhat limited.

Each state library has at a minimum a good selection of that state's records – vital statistics, copies (microfilms) of the US Censuses for that state, etc. See Appendix B for a listing of state libraries.

County Libraries

If you have the opportunity to visit the county library for the place where your ancestor(s) lived, you are most likely in for a treat. Some of my most pleasant genealogical memories are associated with prowling through county libraries. As with state libraries, county libraries are constrained by the budgeting that they have received. But I have found some wonderful nuggets in the county libraries I have done research in through the years.

Often, these libraries contain books of biographies that list the *Who's Who* of the counties – early pioneers, politicians, philanthropists, civil servants, etc. While your ancestors may not have been one of the founding fathers of the country, they may have played an important role in the early days of their county's development. You may also find old county newspapers, indexed obituaries, deed books, maps, wills, etc. that will assist you in your search for your ancestors.

One county library deserves special attention here. The Allen County Library in Fort Wayne, Indiana has been obsessed with maintaining and

---

POIGNANT DISCOVERY

I knew that my 3rd great grandfather had served as a Colonel in the Civil War under Ulysses S. Grant, and I also knew that he was killed in a skirmish just prior to the Siege of Vicksburg. But I was unprepared for the article I found in his hometown newspaper:

Colonel Horney Killed!

"A private letter written to a gentleman in St. Louis, Missouri from Vicksburg under the date May 20th, and published in Monday morning's Democrat, gives the sad news that Colonel Leonidas Horney, of the 10th Missouri Regiment, was killed before Vicksburg. This is indeed bitter news to his family and many friends in this county. Let us hope the intelligence may not be confirmed."

Unfortunately, the intelligence was indeed confirmed. As an officer in the Civil War, the death of this small-town war hero had been an important event in the history of this town.

---

expanding its outstanding genealogical collection. Their collection is considered one of the most exceptional in the nation.

The Allen County Library set the standard for the genealogical world by developing an exhaustive index of genealogical articles that have been published in periodicals since 1847. The index covers subjects, surnames and locations. Called *PERSI* (*PERiodical Source Index*), it is a wonderful tool.

The Allen County Library has launched a website that might be of interest to you: www.acpl.lib.in.us/genealogy/genealogy.html. Check it out - you just might find something that will assist you in finding that latest elusive ancestor you are seeking.

Genealogical and Historical Society Libraries
Many genealogical societies and state historical societies have collections of books, maps, deeds, and other materials that may be available for you to research. Often, those collections center on the surname and major branches off that surname that the genealogical organization is dedicated to researching. These societies often go to great lengths to locate and purchase books that contain information about the family. They may have also published books on your ancestors.

Some genealogical and historical societies lend their books out – in other words, they allow them to be taken from the premises just like a regular library. Others participate in the inter-library loan process, wherein individuals can request a book or microfilm from a library in another location and have it shipped to their local library. If you are planning a trip to a distant library, check to see if the book you are hoping to review is there before you go (it may be loaned out); a phone call to the library should answer the question.

University Libraries
All universities and colleges have libraries, and many of them have genealogy collections. Don't pass these up without a look. They are often the source of valuable genealogical information. I have spent many enjoyable and profitable hours in university libraries scouting for clues about my ancestors.

National Archives
There are fourteen locations of the National Archives geographically dispersed around the United States. Each contains a treasure trove of

genealogical information, including all the US Censuses that are available for the public to view. Following are their locations:

Alaska
654 West Third Avenue
Anchorage, Alaska 99501-2145
Tel. 907/271-2441
E-mail: alaska.archives@nara.gov
Website: www.archives.gov/facilities/ak/anchorage.html

California
24000 Avila Road,
1st Floor, East Entrance
Laguna Niguel, California 92677-3497
Tel. 949/360-2641
E-mail: laguna.archives@nara.gov
Website: www.archives.gov/facilities/ca/laguna_niguel.html

1000 Commodore Drive
San Bruno, California 94066-2350
Tel. 650/876-9009
E-mail: sanbruno.archives@nara.gov
Website: www.archives.gov/facilities/ca/san_francisco.html

Colorado
Bldg. 48, Denver Federal Center
West 6th Avenue and Kipling Street
Denver, Colorado 80225-0307
Tel. 303/236-0806
E-mail: denver.archives@nara.gov
Website: www.archives.gov/facilities/co/denver.html

Georgia
1557 St. Joseph Avenue
East Point, Georgia 30344-2593
Tel. 404/763-7474
E-mail: atlanta.center@nara.gov
Website: www.archives.gov/facilities/ga/atlanta.html

Illinois
7358 South Pulaski Road
Chicago, Illinois 60629-5898
Tel. 773/581-7816

E-mail: chicago.archives@nara.gov
Website: www.archives.gov/facilities/il/chicago.html

Massachusetts
Frederick C. Murphy Federal Center
380 Trapelo Road
Waltham, Massachusetts 02452-6399
Tel. 781/647-8104
Tel. 866/406-2379
E-mail: waltham.center@nara.gov
Website: www.archives.gov/facilities/ma/boston.html

10 Conte Drive
Pittsfield, Massachusetts 01201-8230
Tel. 413/445-6885
E-mail: archives@pittsfield.nara.gov
Website: www.archives.gov/facilities/ma/pittsfield.html

Missouri
2312 East Bannister Road
Kansas City, Missouri 64131-3011
Tel. 816/926-6920
E-mail: kansascity.archives@nara.gov
Website: www.archives.gov/facilities/mo/kansas_city.html

New York
201 Varick Street
New York, New York 10014-4811
Tel. 212/337-1300
E-mail: newyork.archives@nara.gov
Website: www.archives.gov/facilities/ny/new_york_city.html

Pennsylvania
900 Market Street
Philadelphia, Pennsylvania 19107-4292
Tel. 215/597-3000
E-mail: philadelphia.archives@nara.gov
Website: www.archives.gov/facilities/pa/philadelphia_center_city.html

Texas
501 West Felix Street, Building 1
Fort Worth, Texas 76115-3405
Tel. 817/334-5525, ext. 243

E-mail: ftworth.archives@nara.gov
Website: www.archives.gov/facilities/tx/fort_worth.html

Washington
6125 Sand Point Way NE
Seattle, Washington 98115-7999
Tel. 206/526-6501
E-mail: seattle.archives@nara.gov
Website: www.archives.gov/facilities/wa/seattle.html

Washington DC
National Archives Building
700 Pennsylvania Avenue, N.W.
Washington DC
Tel. 866/272-6272
Website: www.archives.gov/

Hours vary from center to center. Generally, all offices are open Monday through Friday during normal business hours. Most offer at least one evening a week when they are open until 8:00pm and most are also open at least one if not two Saturdays per month.

So – you might ask, "Okay – so these are the addresses to the National Archives. What does that mean to me, and in particular, how will it assist my genealogical research?" Good question. The National Archives are a treasure trove of genealogical information, if you just know how to access it. For example, the following types of genealogical resources are available to you at the National Archives:

•Bounty Land Warrant records
•Census Records (1790 – 1930)
•Immigration Records
•Income Tax Records of the Civil War Years
•Land Records
•Military Records
•Naturalization Records
•Passenger Lists
•Passport Applications
•Pension Records
•Social Security Records
•Vital Records

The National Archives Records Administration Department (NARA) offers you a website that will help you learn what kinds of records are available at their facilities. If you surf to the NARA catalogs website: www.archives.gov/research_room/media_formats/microfilm.html, you'll find a list of on-line card catalogs. Here are a few of them:

•Genealogical and Biographical Research: A Select Catalog of NARA Microfilm Publications
•The Federal Population Censuses: Catalogs of NARA Microfilm
•Immigration and Passenger Lists: A Select Catalog of NARA Microfilm Publications
•Military Service Records: A Select Catalog of NARA Microfilm Publications
•American Indians: A Select Catalog of NARA Microfilm Publications
•Black Studies: A Select Catalog of NARA Microfilm Publications
•Diplomatic Records: A Select Catalog of NARA Microfilm Publications
•Federal Court Records: A Select Catalog of NARA Microfilm Publications
•Microfilm Pamphlets and Roll Lists
•Microfilm Publication M1131: Records of Appointment of Postmasters, Oct. 1789-1832. 4 rolls
•Microfilm Publication M1845: Card Records of Headstones Provided for Deceased Union Civil War Veterans, ca. 1879-ca. 1903. 22 rolls.
•Microfilm Publication T288: General Index to Pension Files, 1861-1934 (544 rolls).

Each entry above includes links to other websites that provide much more information on just what is available, how to access the information, etc.

The NARA website is worth a bit of your time to familiarize yourself with the information that is available. Unfortunately, very little of the information contained in the National Archives system is available on-line. Add to that the fact that you don't live within easy driving distance of one of the National Archives locations. What's a genealogist to do? Never fear – there is another way to access many of the records the National Archives owns other than visiting one of their locations. You may either purchase microfilms ($34 each) or more practical – you can rent them. Here are the rental rates as of this writing:

1 to 4 rolls — $3.50 per roll
5 to 9 rolls — $3.00 per roll
10 or more rolls — $2.50 per roll

Shipping is $5.00 for 1 to 9 rolls, and $10.00 for 10 or more rolls. You may keep these rolls for one month, and may extend the rental for one additional month by paying an additional $3.50 per roll.

What? You don't have a microfilm reader in your basement? No worries – there are over 6,000 libraries in the United States that have microfilm readers you can use, as well as the local Family History Centers of the LDS Church.

For an interesting tour, go to the National Archives website at www.archives.gov/research_room/genealogy/research_topics.html. Each of the above areas is listed (along with others), and each has a link to more information about the records that are available to research. Unfortunately, very little genealogical information is available on-line; this site just serves as something of a card catalog to help you find what is available at which of the National Archive sites.

The Hunt Begins!
So you have located a library that has a genealogical section, and you are hoping to find out something about an ancestor or two. What kinds of records might you find, and what kind of information can you hope to glean from those records? Following are a few of the more common types of records you may find. Remember that many of these records may be secondary resources of information, as the information may have been recorded years after an event occurred.

Vital Statistics Records
Many libraries have compendiums of information about births, deaths and marriages that took place within their city, county and/or state. Many times, local genealogical societies have gone to local government offices and gleaned and indexed information about these important genealogical events.

Census Records
Every state library and many county and local libraries have copies of the federal censuses that were conducted for their community. The state library will have copies of the census for the state, and city and county libraries may have them for the entire state or maybe just for the city or county they serve. A phone call to the library before going allows you to find out just what they have available in this area. See Chapter 11 for more on census research.

In addition to the US Census, many local censuses may have been taken that will shed light on your ancestors. Population, agricultural and other censuses may have been taken through the years in the community where your ancestor lived.

Biographies
I have had great success in finding biographies of several ancestors. Sometimes they are listed in *Who's Who* books of the city, county or state where they lived. I am not descended from royalty (few of us are), but at least a few of my ancestors played important roles in their communities, such as county surveyors, justices of the peace, businessmen, teachers, etc. Perhaps some of your ancestors did the same. Look for biographies, county and state histories. Most of these books have indexes or tables of contents that will allow you to quickly ascertain whether one of your ancestors is included.

Obituaries
Many library genealogy sections keep records of printed obituaries for the inhabitants of the community they serve. Some of these are kept alphabetically, some chronologically and indexed, or a combination of both. Obituaries are rich sources of clues. Following are information tidbits I have gleaned from obituaries through the years:

- Death date and place
- Burial date and place
- Birth date and place
- Names of parents
- Names of spouse and children
- Married names of daughters
- Places of residence of parents
- Places of residence of grown children
- Names of siblings
- Names of grandparents, aunts and uncles
- Address at time of death
- Occupation
- When they moved to the town/county/state
- Where they moved from
- Military service

When searching for obituaries, be creative. If the library doesn't have an indexed book of obituaries, do they have microfilms of old newspapers? If you know the approximate year of death, you can scan the obituary sections of weekly newspapers for several years pretty quickly. Several years ago I was looking for the obituary of a great uncle who lived in southern Colorado. I found out what newspapers were published in his small community (actually – in a small community nearby) and began searching.

I realized very quickly that the first newspaper of each year carried a list of all the deaths of county residents the previous year, along with their date of death. That allowed me to home in very quickly on the specific weekly edition I needed to search. I was able to find a ton of previously unknown genealogical information not only on him, but about his parents and several uncles. These clues allowed me to find more information about each of these individuals at a later date.

If you copy the information in an obituary, or even if you obtain a copy of the obituary, be sure and include the date the obituary appeared, and the name of the newspaper.

As a record of death, obituaries can be considered a primary genealogical source; as far as birth information it may contain, it is a secondary source.

Old Newspapers
Old newspapers from the community where your ancestors lived can provide a rich source of information and clues about your ancestors. As mentioned earlier, obituaries are found there, as well as human interest stories, classified ads, old advertisements, and interesting articles about the history of our country, especially during the time of presidential elections and wartime. These give you a flavor for what your ancestors were experiencing. And perhaps you'll discover the profession of your ancestor in an advertisement or an article about him or her.

Other information that might be found in a local newspaper includes:

•Obituaries
•Birth announcements
•Engagement or wedding announcements
•Visiting family members (out-of-town visitors were big news for local newspapers to report!)
•Notices of estate sales
•Property sales
•Letters to the editor
•Records of religious events: weddings, christenings, Bar or Bat Mitzvahs, etc.

Land Records
Many libraries contain records of land deals, surveys, deeds issued, etc. This information may not tell you an ancestor's birth date, but it may confirm that he or she lived in this community. It may also provide clues to aunts, uncles, grandparents, etc. that were living nearby. Often, I have found that land traded hands between family members.

City Telephone Directories
I have used city directories to help confirm the existence of an ancestor in that community at a certain time. I have also used it as a clue to indicate when an ancestor died or moved from the area. Once I found an obituary listing that mentioned a 2nd great uncle of mine – before that, I had no idea that he had lived in the area. The obituary indicated that this great uncle, who had been a relative of the deceased, had moved to the Portland area. I was able to use old city telephone directories to find out when he arrived in the area, and I learned when he left. That gave me an approximate year to begin searching in Portland for clues about this individual's arrival. A subsequent search enabled me to locate the individual in Portland.

Some city directories include a householders index, which listed the addresses that people were living at. This allowed me to locate individuals who were living with my relatives. In one case, it was a mother-in-law, in another it was a daughter and son-in-law of my ancestor.

Histories
Many libraries have histories – community as well as biographical – of the communities where they are located. These books can provide information about early settlers and prominent citizens. Keep an eye out: many of these books contain photos of the individuals whose biographies are contained therein. This may be the first glimpse of what the ancestor you are searching for looked like. For earlier generations, before photography was generally available, you may find a drawing of the individual.

Again – recognize that these books are secondary sources of information – to be used for clues to help you find primary sources.

Cemetery Indexes
Many genealogical libraries contain indexes for all the cemeteries in the communities they serve. These can be valuable, as they will help you identify where you might go to look at and take pictures of tombstones. Often, the books will give you the exact location of a tombstone.

Befriend the Librarian!

Spend a few minutes and get to know the librarian that is familiar with the genealogy section of the library you go to. Then don't be afraid to ask him or her about your search. If you explain what you're looking for, he or she may have suggestions about special collections the library has, or expedited ways to find what you are looking for. They will know whether special censuses were taken that might yield a clue to your ancestors, or whether certain records are available at the library to assist you in your search.

Collections & Libraries Checklist

Before going to the library in search of your ancestors, do or bring the following:

___ Determine who you are looking for.

___ What information do you want to find? Be open to other information you may run across.

___ Bring all the information you have about the person you are seeking: approximate birth dates and place, parents' names, etc.

___ Materials to record information: pens or pencils, pad of paper, family group sheets, etc.

___ Record the date you were in the library.

___ Record the name and address of the library you visited.

___ Record the information sources you searched through (it may be years until you return; no sense going through records you already searched!)

___ Record any information you find completely and accurately, including information about the source that provided the information.

___ Make copies of articles or microfilm pages that contain genealogical information.

___ Engage the librarian in your search; he or she may know of resources you hadn't thought of.

___ Be curious! Snoop through information sources that might contain additional information.

Additional Resources
Greenwood, Val D., *The Researcher's Guide to American Genealogy*, Genealogical Publishing Company, 2nd edition (April 1990)

Luebking, Sandra H. (Editor) and Eichholz, Alice, *The Source: A Guide of American Genealogy*, Ancestry Publishing (May 1997)

Mills, Elizabeth Shown, *Evidence! : Citation & Analysis for the Family Historian,* Genealogical Publishing Company (January 2000)

Guide to Genealogical Research in the National Archives, Church of Jesus Christ of Latter-day Saints.

9. COMPUTERS & THE INTERNET

It's safe to say that the computer and the Internet are the two greatest aids to genealogical research to date.

While computers have been a boon to the business world, they have also opened up wide avenues for genealogists. Computer software has been designed to assist genealogists in keeping track of the legions of ancestors that they have searched out and identified, providing handy and efficient ways of grouping them into families and then displaying them, either on the screen or on paper.

The advent and proliferation of e-mail has also been a remarkable aid to genealogists. Communication about families that once took weeks or months now often takes moments, as information is often requested and exchanged in a matter of minutes. I have personally benefited from the use of e-mail in my genealogical research, as I have made and kept contact with individuals who are working on several of my lines.

The Internet

As wonderful as the computer is for organizing ancestral files and facilitating communication with others working on your family lines, perhaps its greatest genealogical value is in providing a gateway to the Internet. The Internet is a powerful tool that enables genealogists to research records located literally anywhere in the world. Formerly, many of these records were virtually unavailable to genealogists simply because of the expense that would have been incurred in traveling to distant locations to view the records. But that is no longer the case. Many of those records are available on-line, and are only a mouse click or two away from researchers.

To illustrate the power I speak of, try this experiment: Go to the Internet, and using whichever search engine you are most familiar with (Yahoo!,

COMPUTERS & THE INTERNET

Lycos, AltaVista, Excite, Hotbot, Infoseek, etc.), type in your last name (or the last name of an ancestor) and the word *genealogy*, and click on *Search*. I did this for a number of my lines, and here are the number of hits I came up with for each (a "hit" is Internet lingo for "how many websites were found with the information you requested"):

•Cunningham – 8
•Horney – 32
•Hudson – 12
•Lowrance – 1,070
•McCollough – 401
•Phillips – 13
•Quillen – 1
•Ritchey – 4,100
•Sellers – 2
•Stunkard – 50
•Throckmorton – 2
•Turpin – 1

Each one of these hits has the potential of yielding information about a family member for whom you have been searching in vain. And more often than not, the information doesn't stop there – my experience is that once I find one person in this manner, there are often two, three or more generations beyond that included in the listing.

Genealogy Websites
There are literally tens of thousands, perhaps hundreds of thousands of websites devoted to genealogical research, all just a mouse click away. The Internet is the largest genealogy library in the world. Listed below are some of my favorite and most productive websites, and a little about each of them.

Cyndi's List of Genealogy Sites on the Internet (www.cyndislist.com). When you think of Cyndi's List, you should think of a mammoth card catalog in the sky - it is a gigantic index of genealogical websites. When you go to Cyndi's List, one of the first things you see will be the number of active links available through Cyndi's List. It seems that every time I log onto Cyndi's List, the number of websites grows. At the time of this writing, the number of links is 240,200! Now that's a lot of websites.

In addition to being an index, Cyndi's List provides links to each website listed, so once you find a website that catches your interest, you merely click on the link and you are there. It is remarkably user friendly, and is a great place to begin your on-line research. If there is a weakness on Cyndi's List, it is the many, many website links that are there. You'll be like a kid in a candy store, bedazzled and unsure where to turn next. Earlier in this chapter I suggested you enter the word *genealogy* along with your surname, or the surname for one of your ancestors, into a search engine and see how many hits you could get. I entered the same surnames again on Cyndi's List, and here are the number of hits I got for each name:

	Yahoo!	**Cyndi's List**
Cunningham	8	2,750
Horney	32	68
Hudson	12	3,373
Lowrance	1,070	116
McCollough	401	216
Phillips	13	6,182
Quillen	1	161
Ritchey	4,100	1,524
Sellers	2	1,384
Stunkard	50	12
Throckmorton	2	287
Turpin	1	601

(Note: To get to these Cyndi's List pages, I entered *Personal Home Pages* in the box on the home page of Cyndi's list. Then I selected any of the personal home pages that were displayed. At the bottom left-hand side of each personal home page is an alphabet for you to begin spelling the surnames you are looking for.)

Some of these hits are websites containing information about each surname. Others are links to message boards where people leave information about individuals, or leave queries about individuals ("Can anyone provide me information about my 2nd great grandfather Jonathan Baldwin Quillen? I think he was born in..."), and a host of other sites of genealogical value.

I guarantee that you will find something of genealogical interest if you visit Cyndi's List. As you learn to work with it and navigate around, you will be amazed at the wide variety of resources that are available there. Below are just a few of the many categories that are available on Cyndi's List:

•**African American** – tools to assist you in doing genealogical research for African American ancestors.

•**Austria** – If your ancestors came from Austria, here is good place to begin your search for them.

•**Births and Baptisms** – lists of vital records (birth, marriage, death) for a number of states.

•**Catholic** – links to many Catholic genealogical sources. The Catholic Church has been a prolific recorder of important and vital genealogical information for centuries.

•**Eastern Europe** – So your ancestors came from countries formerly behind the Iron Curtain? Don't despair – there are dozens of links that will help you begin or enhance your search.

•**Death Records** – Have you had any ancestors die? Many of them may be waiting to be found in the nearly 500 death record links available here.

•**Handwriting and Script** – several dozen links to resources that will help you decipher those sometimes-unintelligible scribbles on genealogical records.

•**Hispanic, Central and South America, and the West Indies** – there are over 400 links dealing with individuals from this part of the world.

•**How-To** – now that you have this book, you'll have less need for these sites, although you may glean a nugget or two.

•**Immigration and Naturalization** – here are over 300 sites that will help you find those intrepid ancestors who left all to come to America.

•**Jewish** – nearly 400 links that focus on your Jewish roots.

•**Military Resources Worldwide** – the military often kept detailed records of its members, including family relationships.

•**Native American** – over 300 links assist those researching their Native American roots.

•**Obituaries** – over 250 links that might help you find the obituary of some ancestor. Obituaries are often a rich source of genealogical information.

•**Prisons, Prisoners and Outlaws** – yes, most of us have a few horse thieves in our ancestry!

•**Professional Researchers, Volunteers and Other Research Services** – over 800 links that may provide possible options to help you clamber over genealogical stumbling blocks.

•**Surnames, Family Associations and Newsletters** – nearly 5,500 family and genealogical organizations that may help you with your research.

•**Western Europe** – if you are like most Americans, you'll benefit from the many links that will assist you in doing research in this region of the world.

•**Wills and Probate** – another rich source of genealogical information when all else has failed.

· The above list barely scratches the surface of what you will find on Cyndi's List. I guarantee you will find Cyndi's List to be most helpful and intriguing.

Ellis Island website. If your ancestors came to America between 1892 and 1924, you'll definitely want to check out www.ellisisland.org, the official website for that immigration gateway into the United States. During that time, more than 12 million individuals were processed through her gates, all headed for the freedoms America offered.

Before you can do much on the website, you must register. This is a relatively painless (and free) process that takes all of one or two minutes. Once registered, you'll be able to tour around and see most of the information available on the website.

The most robust feature of the website is the *Passenger Search*, which allows you to search for your ancestor among the 22 million passengers whose names were on passenger lists (also called *ship manifests*) of ships that arrived at Ellis Island. These individuals may have been passengers, immigrants or crew members who arrived in America between 1892 and 1924. Volunteers spent years microfilming, transcribing, cataloging and indexing the information for the Ellis Island Foundation. And now the information is available to you.

Getting information from the website is quite easy. From the home page of ellisisland.org, click on *Passenger Search*, then click on *New Search* on the page that appears. On the next page, type the first and last names (at least the last name) of the ancestor you are looking for, indicate whether they are male or female, and then click on *Continue*.

Let's use an example. The original spelling of my surname was McQuillan, and my ancestors came to America from the area that is now Northern Ireland. If I enter the name McQuillan in the required box and click *Continue*, I learn that 335 people with the surname McQuillan were listed on passenger lists between 1892 and 1924. The first page lists the first 25 individuals that were found. The list includes the names of the passengers, their residence, the year they arrived, and their age on arrival. Since my family is from Northern Ireland, I scan the list looking for people whose residence is listed as being from Ireland. The first page tells me that a Philip McQuillan came to America from Belfast, Ireland (Northern Ireland did not exist as an entity until 1922) in 1915. Clicking on his name (which is linked to his passenger record), the following information appears:

Name: Philip McQuillan
Ethnicity: Britain
Place of Residence: Belfast, Ireland
Date of Arrival: October 31, 1915
Age on Arrival: 33 years
Gender: Male
Marital Status: Single
Ship of Travel: New York
Port of Departure: Liverpool, England

While this summary does not contain primary genealogical source information, it has a number of secondary information tidbits that might be of use to me as I search for more information about this possible ancestor. It tells me his place of residence was Belfast. It tells me he was 33 in 1915, which translates to an approximate birth date of 1881 or 1882. (Assuming he wasn't fibbing about his age, he would have been born in 1882 if his birthday was before October 31, or in 1881 if his birthday was between November 1 and December 31.) It tells me that he was single, and that he departed from Liverpool, England. That last tidbit is interesting. There were a number of Irish ports that transatlantic ships departed from (Queenstown / Cobh, Belfast, Derry), but he departed from Liverpool, England. That tells me that even though he considered his residence as Belfast, he may have been working in England (as many of his fellow countrymen did – and still do).

On the same page where this information is displayed, there are two nice options, especially if you know or believe this passenger is an ancestor. If you click on the button that says *View Original Ship Manifest*, you will be taken to a page with a photograph of the actual passenger list where your ancestor's name is written. The picture can be enlarged (look for the small icon of a magnifying glass), and a veritable genealogical treasure awaits you. The ship's manifest collected an amazing (and sometimes startling!) set of facts about the individual, including some wonderful genealogical clues. Many of the questions are similar to those found on the US Census. The ship manifest questions changed somewhat from year to year, but regardless of the year they provide interesting information on each passenger. In 1915, the questions asked (and answered) were:

•Were they a citizen, diplomat, tourist, or a citizen of Canada, China or Mexico?
•What was their age in years and months?
•What was their sex and marital status?
•What was their occupation, and could they read and write?
•What was their nationality and race?
•What was their last permanent address?
•What was the name and complete residence address of a relative or friend in the country from whence they came?
•What was the passenger's final destination (state and town)?
•Did they have a ticket to their final destination?
•Who paid the passage for this individual?
•Did they have at least $50? If not, how much did they have?
•Had they been to the United States before, and if so, where and for how long?
•Were they coming to visit a relative or friend? And if so, who was it and what was their full address?
•Were they a polygamist?
•Were they an Anarchist?
•What was their mental and physical health condition?
•Were they deformed or crippled, and if so, the nature, length of time and cause?
•Did they have any identifying marks?
•What was their height, complexion and color of hair and eyes?
•Where was their place of birth?

You can see why some of this information would make a genealogist's heart flutter! In the case of Philip McQuillan, in addition to what we learned on the summary page (his age, marital status, residence, and place of departure), we learn that he was:

•a dairyman;
•from Belfast;
•the son of William McQuillan of Fairview Glen Road in Belfast;
•going to see his brother, James McQuillan, who lived on Liberty Avenue
    in Pittsburgh, Pennsylvania;
•not a polygamist or anarchist (thank goodness!);
•had no "deformities" or identifying marks;
•5'-3" with a light complexion, brown hair and blue eyes;
•born in Belfast.

Wow! What a wonderful (secondary) source of genealogical information. From the ship's manifest we learned the approximate year of his birth, the name of his father, the fact that he had a brother named James who lived in Pittsburgh, and that Philip was born in Belfast.

From this information, I have more information that will help me do research not only on James, but also for his father William and his brother James.

For a few dollars you can receive a copy of the original passenger list. An 11"x17" copy will cost you $25, and a 17"x22" copy will cost you $35. Caution: the ship's manifest was kept in large log books, and to get all the information, you would have to purchase both pages that the information extended over, so the entire cost would be double the above prices. But if this were truly an ancestor, what a prize to have a copy of! Also available to view and/or purchase is a photograph of the ship that your ancestor came to America in. Back on the web page that listed the summary of the passenger's information is a label entitled *View Ship*. Just click on that label and *voila* – there is the picture of the ship. You may also purchase this picture for $10.00 or $12.50, depending on whether you want a 5"x7" or 9"x12" picture. Again, I think this would be a wonderful thing to have for an ancestor.

As you search for ancestors on the website, you are given the opportunity to save any searches that you are conducting, so you capture all the information as you go along. That way, if your research trips are hours, days or weeks (or months!) apart, you don't have to replow old ground.

The Ellis Island website also provides a nice opportunity to start a *Family Scrapbook*. Accessed via an icon on the Ellis Island home page, this section of the website allows you to create an on-line scrapbook for your ancestors. You may add stories, photos and other information about your ancestors and have it be included in the Ellis Island Family History Archive. To access this section and create your family scrapbook, you need to become a "sustaining member" of The Statue of Liberty-Ellis Island Foundation. A one-year membership costs $45.00. The membership fee enables the organization to continue to provide a number of great services to visitors to Ellis Island – those who come in person as well as those who are virtual visitors.

All immigrants who came to America came through Ellis Island, right? Wrong! Ellis Island was the busiest port of entry (and the one with the best PR agent?) but there were many other entry points into the US, including Baltimore, Detroit, New Orleans, Philadelphia, and San Francisco. This is certainly not an exhaustive list, so don't be discouraged if you don't find your ancestors on any of their passenger lists.

The Ellis Island Foundation lists the following **Five Helpful Hints** to making your search easier on their website and in their database:

1. Is your ancestor's name spelled correctly? Can you think of alternative spellings? As discussed before, sometimes names are spelled differently today than they were in earlier generations. Be open to those possible variations.

2. Even if you know the person's first name, search with just the first initial and last name, or don't use a first name in your search at all. Don't unnecessarily limit the database search. Let's use me for an example. Let's say that I came to the United States through Ellis Island in 1916 (I did not, but play along). My name is William Daniel Quillen. Let's say my descendant knew that, so searched for William Quillen. No luck. Then they searched for Bill Quillen (a natural next step). No luck. Then they tried W. Quillen. No luck. Finally, out of desperation they try leaving my first name and initial out of the search completely. That search turns up one Daniel Quillen – me! Little did they know – 90 years after I immigrated here – that I went by my middle name and not my first name. Had they simply used my first name or the initial from my first name, they would never have found me. So close, yet so far away!

3. Most manifests are actually two pages, not one. The most important is the first page, with the passenger's name on the far left

side. Make certain you are looking at the right page – sometimes the second page comes up first! Click the button that looks like a magnifying glass to enlarge the screen view of the manifest. Scroll to the left side until you find passenger names; then you know you are in the right place! If there are no passenger names on the left side of the page you are looking at, then close the window and click on either the *Previous* or *Next* button to get to the appropriate page. Don't come this far and then give up because you were looking at the wrong page!

4. These records are not a perfect collection. Sometimes you may not find an ancestor's name where the database says it should be on a particular page. If that is the case, try clicking on the *Previous* or *Next* buttons and scanning those pages. The name you are seeking may very well be close by.

5. Don't get discouraged! Well, that goes without saying.

The Hamburg Passenger Lists
Moving from *immigration* records as a source of genealogical research, let's next consider *emigration* records. (Hint: Remember *I*nto for *I*mmigration and *E*xit for *E*migration!) The Hamburg passenger lists are a rich source of information about several million Europeans who came to America through Hamburg between 1850 and 1934 (few records were kept during the years of World War I, 1915 – 1919). The nationalities are heavily slanted toward Germans, but individuals from central and eastern Europe also used Hamburg as their point of departure to America and other points. In fact, it is estimated that nearly one-third of the people who emigrated from central and eastern Europe used Hamburg as their jumping-off place.

Because the emigrants who came through Hamburg are predominantly German, you'll find the Hamburg Passenger Lists treated quite extensively in the German section of the Ethnic Research chapter.

FamilyToolbox.net. FamilyToolbox.net is another of the major genealogy websites that serves as a card catalog (or *toolbox*, if you wish) of genealogy sites on the Internet. At the time of this writing, it did not have nearly as many sites as Cyndislist.com, but it organized itself in an entirely different manner. While I did not find it as intuitive as Cyndi's List, other researchers like it better.

It contains links to a variety of genealogical resources, such as bulletin boards, mailing lists, query boards, computer software for genealogy and other topics of interest to genealogists.

One of the features I like about FamilyToolbox.net is that throughout the website, there are many helpful links that provide advice on a wide variety of topics. These might be information about the latest edition of genealogy software that has come out, or new records that the government has made available, articles on a specific research topic, etc.

FamilyToolbox.net is sponsored by businesses that target genealogists. That sponsorship takes the form of frequent advertisements that pop up on the screen, and many of the screens have static advertisements on them. While these are sometimes helpful, I generally find them a bit blatant and annoying. Cindi's List also has a few advertisements, but they are not as intrusive as on this website. FamilyToolbox.net also can also be accessed via www.genealogytoolbox.com.

Random Acts of Genealogical Kindness – this is one of my favorite genealogy sites on the Internet! I think it symbolizes the values of genealogical generosity that most genealogists are known for. The website is www.raogk.org, and I guarantee you will find it to your liking.

The premise is this: thousands of genealogists offer their time and research talents to do research for other genealogists who live in other parts of the world. For example, a genealogist in Hemmingen, Germany might volunteer to do a variety of genealogy-related research projects for anyone needing that research. They might go check out a nearby cemetery, searching for specific surnames. Or they might go to the local magistrate's office to review a marriage log book, or a local parish to scan the birth and baptismal registry from 100 years ago. The organization asks its members to donate at least one search a month, for which they receive no pay. If you want someone to do some research for you, you need to volunteer to do at least one search for someone else. The only cost to the requesting genealogist is for specific costs related to the search: photocopying, gas (if the search is done far from the researcher), etc.

What a great site.

Databases are a boon to genealogists. Think of a huge file cabinet – almost infinite in size, with file drawer after file drawer. It might seem overwhelming to try and find anything in all those drawers. But through the power of the Internet, you can find names of ancestors with just a few key strokes. The names contained in all those file drawers are computerized and compiled in a way that it is easy to find whoever it is you are looking for.

One such database that you will become fond of is RootsWeb – www.rootsweb.com. Here is the mission statement of the RootsWeb website: *The primary purpose and function of RootsWeb.com is to connect people so that they can help each other and share genealogical research.* And from what I can judge, they are successful in their mission. This powerful database provides search capabilities, on-line message boards, e-mail lists, the opportunity to input your own genealogical information for the benefit others, and even family trees. Considered one of the largest and most user-friendly databases, RootsWeb boasts over 372 million names that you can search through. Take a few moments and just putter around in it – you will be surprised at the power and information that will be at your very fingertips.

Let's take a short and quick tour of the RootsWeb website:

Once you have typed in the RootWeb address in your browser (www.rootsweb.com), you'll come to the RootsWeb home page. Across the top you'll see a toolbar listing the following options:

•Home
•Searches
•Family Trees
•Mailing Lists
•Message Boards
•Websites
•Passwords
•Help

Let's start by clicking on *Searches*. Once you do that, you'll be brought to the *Searches* home page. Just for grins, enter the name of an ancestor that you know a little information about. That way, you'll be able to see how quickly you can get lots of useful information. I typed in the name of my elusive great-grandfather, Edgar Quillen. Almost instantaneously I was informed that his name had been located in 4 of 46 databases searched: World Connect, Social Security Death Index, the Roots Surname List, and a database of living individuals (which I can ignore, since he has been gone for many years).

I click on the World Connect choice, which tells me that there were 13 individuals named Edgar that they found in their database. A quick scan and I find my great-grandfather:

	Birth / Christening		Death / Burial		Database Order Records	Other Matches
	Date	Place	Date	Place		
Quillen, Edgar Estill					:2284453	Census Newpapers Histories
Father: Jonathan Baldwin Quillen Mother: Sarah Burke						

Even though the middle name is misspelled Estill instead of Estil, I am reasonably certain this is my great-grandfather, especially because the parents listed for him match my records. Other records had birth and death places listed for the individuals, but whoever shared this information apparently didn't know this information.

But who did share this information? If I click on the *Database* listed – in this case :2284453, I am taken to a page that lists the e-mail address of the submitter. Now I can contact him and see what other information he may have. Or better yet, I can update him with the information that I have that he may not have.

Okay, next let's check out another area of the website. At the top toolbar, click on *Family Trees*. Enter the name you are looking for, and it will take you to a similar table as the one listed above.

Now let's check out the *Mailing Lists* section. Once you click on that, you'll be given numerous options. You can go to any of the following genealogical mailing lists:

•Surnames
•USA (by state)
•International (by country)
•Other (general information on a host of topics)

From this point, you can also access Roots-L, a mailing list that will unite you with something like 85,000 other users across the world who are actively asking for and sharing genealogy information.

Back to the *Mailing Lists* section. If you click on *Surnames*, you'll have the opportunity to click on the first letter of the surname of the ancestor you are seeking, and you'll be taken to a list of the surnames that have e-mail traffic / queries, etc. Quickly scan the list and see if there is any information on the surname you are researching. A quick trip there will reveal anyone who is doing research on the same surname, and their questions and (hopefully) answers they received from others. Here is an item I found, which is typical of others in this section:

> *I am looking for information on James W. Quillen/Quillin and his sister Lizzie D. Quillen/Quillin (who married John T. Robertson). Their parents were Timothy Allen Quillen/Quillin and Sarah Katherine Denton - Quillen/Quillin. If they sound familiar please email me.*
>
> *Thanks,*
>
> *Mary*

Note: Mary had been answered by an individual who indicated that he had some ancestors named Timothy Quillen, and he offered to share whatever information he had to see if there was a tie-in.

The next section to peruse is the *Message Boards* section. Clicking on that title will take you to a page where you can either type in the name you are looking for, or you can refine your search by searching on the specific message board for your surname – if such a board exists. To search for the specific message board, click on the first letter of the surname you are searching for. Subsequent screens will ask you to continue to identify the specific message board by identifying the next letter in the surname, until finally you get a list of surname message boards. Locate the surname you are looking for, and click on it, and whoosh – you are taken to the messages that have been posted by people doing research on the surname you are doing research for.

Moving along, you can next check out the resources available under the *Web Pages* section of RootsWeb. Clicking on that label on the toolbar takes you to a page which gives you the following choices:

•Regional Resources and Websites
•Surname websites

•Major Projects and Sites hosted by Rootsweb
•Miscellaneous pages

If you are fortunate, the surname you are researching may have a website that will be of interest (and will be informative) to you. Numerous of the surnames I am researching have websites established for them. Take a few minutes (hours) and check out the RootsWeb website – I guarantee it will be an interesting and informative trip through the web pages.

There are a number of genealogy sites that offer advanced research capabilities for those willing to pay a subscription fee. Two of the best known are **Genealogy.com** (www.genealogy.com) and **Ancestry.com** (www.ancestry.com). They are sites that offer subscribers a variety of databases through which they can comb in search of their ancestors. For example, as of this writing, Genealogy.com offers a $99.99 one-year subscription that provides access to their US Census database. Subscribers will be able to view images (photos) of actual census pages. If $99.99 seems a little steep for you, they also offer a monthly subscription for $19.99 per month, which can be canceled with 30 days notice. Genealogy.com's website also includes free online classes, articles and advice from professional genealogists, and an extensive collection of proprietary data.

Other services and databases are also available for a fee, as are a number of CD ROM collections.

As you use these services, be aware that most of the actual research information you would like has a price tag attached to it. There are very effective links and enticements that make you feel like you are going to get your answer, only to find that you are led down a path that ends in an offer to buy a subscription, CD or newsletter that might provide the information you are looking for.

AOL.com – Yes, that Master of E-mail also offers a pretty impressive genealogy website at www.hometown.aol.com/USgenealogy. From that home page, type in a search term such as *Irish Genealogy* or *Hispanic Genealogy* and click on *Search*. You'll be taken to a set of links that match your request – and the hunt is on! There are a wide variety of sites available – many of which are merely links to subscription services such as Genealogy.com and Ancestry.com.

Another area of the AOL-sponsored website that I really like is their Genealogy Forum website (www.genealogyforum.com) that is extremely helpful and quite easy to use.

From the home page, click on any of several topics, and you'll be taken to a link that may be of use to you. For example, click on the *Messages* icon and you'll be taken to a message board where individuals post information about various individuals. Perhaps you'll find one of your ancestors hiding there. Under the same icon, look for *Ethnic Resources*, and you're given a choice of African American, Irish, Hispanic, Huguenot, Jewish and Native American links. Click on any of these, and you'll be whisked to a host of websites specializing in the ethnic research area you specified.

Genealogy Software
There are dozens of software packages available on the market today that will help you keep your genealogical research organized. While notebooks and file folders are fine to get you started, as you progress you'll want to begin saving and organizing your genealogy in a more readily accessible fashion, and genealogy software will help you do that. Genealogy software on the market today allows you to input critical information about your ancestors and then provides very simple ways to retrieve and display the information. Using the information you have input, it will gather your ancestors into families in a heartbeat, produce pedigree charts in the blink of an eye, and provide instant access to the 1,000s of records you may have about your ancestors.

As you begin your search for a software package that will work best for you, you'll be amazed (I am, anyway) by the many clever names of genealogy software programs out there: BirthWrite, Brother's Keeper, Family Ties, Family Treemaker, Family Matters and Relatively Yours, to name a few.

So what should you look for when you finally decide to organize all your manual and paper records into a software program? The first and foremost thing I think is important is user friendliness. No matter how powerful your genealogy program is, or how much storage space it has, if you don't understand how to use it, it is of no real use to you. From a capacity and capability standpoint, most of the major software programs available today are pretty much the same, especially for those who are just beginning their genealogical quest.

I have one caution: be certain that whichever program you choose, whether you are a beginner or not, is capable of **GEDCOM** capability. GEDCOM is an acronym for **GE**nealogical **D**ata **COM**munication. It allows you to share your data with other genealogists, and also allows it to be ported (transferred) to other genealogy programs. If you choose a software program that uses proprietary formatting, you will not be able to share or transfer information except to users who use the same program as you. Fortunately, GEDCOM is a pretty standard default for the software programs on the market today, but it is wise to check to make sure.

One other caution: Be sure and check the computer system requirements before you buy. Do you have the horsepower on your computer to run the program – do you even have the space on your hard drive to install it? Once you open the box, you bought it, and as with all software - no returns allowed!

It would be really nice if you could take the various genealogy software programs on the market for a "test drive" so that you can try it out before purchasing it. Fortunately, many of the more popular genealogy programs on the market today provide a demo version of their software that you can play with on their website.

Following are some of the more popular and capable genealogy programs out there:

Personal Ancestral File, more commonly known as PAF, is produced by the Church of Jesus Christ of Latter-day Saints. The LDS Church pioneered the use of software for storing and retrieving genealogy data with several early DOS versions of PAF.

Now all grown up, the Windows version of PAF is one of the most widely used genealogy software programs today. Although it does not provide as many life events as some other programs, it collects the basic and most critical information: birth, baptism, marriage, death and burial dates for each individual. In addition, each event allows you to enter notes regarding the source of information, or just about anything you would like to add.

This is the software program I currently use. I find it intuitive (that is – I can figure it out myself without having to read the manuals) and it has plenty of storage capability for me.

COMPUTERS & THE INTERNET

PAF is considered the Ford or Chevy of genealogy software programs: while it is not as flashy or elegant as some other models, it provides good, reliable service.

PAF has a nice array of reports and charts available. It can produce, either on screen or on paper, family histories, pedigree charts, family group records, and other reports. It will convert data from former versions of PAF software, so presumably, as new versions of the software are produced the ability to convert the last version of PAF software will be available. PAF allows you to attach a person's picture with their record. It also has the ability to generate HTML Web pages.

There is no demo version of the software available. However, there is no need: PAF is available for free from the LDS Church simply by going to their family history website, www.familysearch.org.™ If you cannot download the software from the Internet, you may also order CD or diskette versions of PAF from their website for as little as $6.00, or by calling the Distribution Center (Tel. 800/537-5950).

A lot of the popularity of PAF derives from its price (free) and the fact that it has TempleReady capabilities, a feature that allows LDS genealogists to prepare their records for temple work.

Family Origins is another popular genealogy software program on the market today. It is available from FormalSoft, Inc. (PO Box 495, Springville, Utah 84663). While PAF might be classed as a Ford or a Chevy, Family Origins is probably more in the Cadillac or BMW class because if its extra features. For example, where PAF allows you to identify the basic facts about each person (name, birth, death, marriage, etc.), Family Origins provides over 50 pre-identified information events, including occupation, religion, graduation dates, divorce, etc. If the need strikes you, you can also create your own information categories. It is also one of the few other programs on the market today that provides TempleReady capabilities for its LDS users. This feature alone guarantees it a significant number of additional sales.

Of all the features Family Origins has, the one that most impresses me is its intuitive and user-friendly interface. Some programs on the market just seem too difficult to use. True, they may have great power, but they also require you (or so it seems) to be a computer programmer to get the most out of them. That isn't the case with Family Origins. Even if this is your first venture into a software program, you should find it relatively easy to use. Yet it also has all the horsepower necessary for really advanced genealogists – a great combination.

Family Origins includes a number of nice printing capabilities, including a broad set of reports and family trees. It also includes the capability to create a multimedia scrapbook by allowing you to attach photographs, sound clips, and video clips to any person, family, place, source, or event. It also has the ability to generate HTML web pages.

While PAF is my sentimental favorite, Family Origins has the horsepower to do some really fun things with your genealogy. (It even has a family reunion organizer with all sorts of tips and planning assists.)

The Family Origins website is www.formalsoft.com, and you can download a working copy of Family Origins from their website. You may keep it for a 15-day free trial. You may order your copy of Family Origins by calling 866/GENEALOGY (866/436-3256). At the time of publication, the cost was $29.95 for the latest version.

Family Treemaker is another of the powerful, popular genealogy software packages on the market. In the past, packages ranged from $49.99 to $99.99, it was a little more expensive than some of the other high-performing packages available. However, at the time of this writing, price pressures and excellent competitive products have brought the cost down to a more modest $29.99 for their latest package. Family Treemaker is available at many retail outlets as well as from its website: www.ftm2005.com.

A rich feature set includes well-regarded charts and a strong website generation capability. You can post some of the charts that are available on the Genealogy.com website for free, thus allowing you to share your findings with others. As with the other software programs reviewed here, Family Treemaker has the reputation of being easy to use and easy to navigate in.

Various packages are offered, with the more expensive packages coming with packs of CDs that contain valuable historical data covering over 1,100 years.

There are several features I like in Family Treemaker. First of all, it has an e-mail storage capability that allows you to store the e-mail addresses of other researchers you are communicating with. Gone are the "yellow stickies" with names and e-mail addresses that plague my desktop. I also like the date calculator that allows me to determine the day of the week for any given date in any given year.

The photo capability is great in Family Treemaker, allowing you to create electronic scrapbooks and then print directly from those scrapbooks. Photos can also be linked to specific ancestors, and source materials (birth, death and marriage certificates, wills, etc.) can be scanned and then linked to a specific event.

Earlier versions of **Ancestral Quest** were once regarded as the Number 1 genealogy software on the market. Other software manufacturers have since put their development efforts in high gear and have caught and in some cases surpassed their capabilities. But they are still a strong competitor, worthy of your consideration. Ancestral Quest was developed by Incline Software (PO Box 95543, South Jordan, UT 84095-0543, 800/ 825-8864 or 801/280-4434). It is available from some retail outlets as well as several websites, including www.softwareoasis.net/dvdz.htm and Ancestral Quest's website at www.ancquest.com. The cost at the time of publication is $37.95 for a CD ROM version.

The documentation that accompanies the product is some of the best on the market, and for those who rely heavily on documentation to learn or feel comfortable with a software product, this is a real selling point. It is relatively easy to use software, especially for basic data entry, printing, etc. But for the more advanced features, the documentation is a huge plus.

Ancestral Quest allows you to attach photos, audio and video clips to individuals in such a manner that allow you to create a memorable multimedia keepsake scrapbook. It also has more than adequate report and charting capabilities, including the production of large (320 inch by 320 inch) wall charts.

One feature that excites many genealogists is Ancestral Quest's PAF compatibility. PAF 3.0 and 4.0 records can be read and edited without importing or conversion. And why not? Software developers from Incline Software (the developers of Ancestral Quest) assisted the LDS Church in their development of PAF. Ancestral Quest 11.0 and later versions can also read PAF 5.0 and later files, but cannot edit them. But what do you do if you need the files edited? Simple – since PAF is free, just download the latest version, edit the required files in PAF, and then move them over to Ancestral Quest! They are also one of the few programs on the market today that has TempleReady capability for LDS users.

SECRETS OF TRACING YOUR ANCESTORS

Ancestral Quest's marketing materials say, "(Ancestral Quest's) format is perfect for the beginner and yet powerful enough for the most advanced genealogist." And I have to agree that it is more than merely marketing hype – they do seem to have been successful in blending ease of use with great power.

Ultimate Family Tree is another of the powerful, popular and user-friendly genealogy programs on the market. Developed and marketed by The Learning Company (88 Rowland Way, Novatao, California 94945. Tel. 415/895-2000), it is considered a very well-rounded software package, garnering high marks from users for its charts, reports and publishing capabilities. It is available from many retail outlets as well as from their website at www.uftree.com.

Ultimate Family Tree offers unlimited personal events (birth, marriage, death, occupation, religion, military service, etc.) for genealogists to use. But its claim to fame is a variety of source citation templates that provide users with easy-to-use templates for the most common source documents. In what has become a fairly standard feature for most genealogy programs, Ultimate Family Tree provides you with the capability to create and launch your own genealogy web page, including scanned photos, audio and video clips, etc.

Sound interesting? Go ahead – take it for a spin before you buy - you may download a free demo version of the software from their website. As of this writing, the latest software version was available for $29.95.

Can you stand one more genealogy software review? Another of the powerful yet affordable genealogy software programs on the market is **Legacy**. It comes standard with many of the features its competitors have, but this software is exceptionally intuitive. I particularly like the way it lays out its various pages – they are easy to read and presented in a manner that are visually appealing and that make sense to me. Legacy allows you to enter millions of names (provided you have the disk space), with multiple events for each person. Add photographs, sound bytes or video clips and you've got a great repository for your family records. Add to that its Internet and web page creation capabilities, along with the ability to print a family book complete with pictures and you have a versatile, powerful software package.

The standard edition is $19.95, and the deluxe edition is $29.95. While there are a few additional features available in the deluxe edition, the main difference is that the standard edition is downloaded from the legacy website (www.legacyfamilytree.com) and the deluxe edition provides its software on CD and provides a User's Guide.

Computer & Internet Checklist

___ Does your computer have Internet capability?

___ Do you have an Internet Service Provider? If not, determine which one best meets your needs and budget.

___ Determine the ancestor or surname you want to research.

___ Do you have any clues about your ancestor that might enable you to find them?
   ___ County, state or country of birth
   ___ Country of immigration?
   ___ Approximate date of immigration?
   ___ Did he serve in the military?
   ___ Etc.

___ Select a software package that meets your needs. (Make sure your computer has the memory, horsepower and right operating system to run it!)

___ Decide whether you want to subscribe to one of the genealogy subscription services (Genealogy.com, Ancestry.com, etc.).

Additional Resources

Colletta, John Philip, *They Came in Ships: A Guide to Finding Your Immigrant Ancestor's Ship*, Ancestry Publishing. (March 1998)

Howells, Cyndi, *Netting Your Ancestors: Genealogical Research on the Internet,* Genealogical Publishing Company. (1999)

McClure, Rhonda, *The Complete Idiot's Guide to Online Genealogy*, Alpha Books, 2nd edition. (January 2002)

Tepper, Michael, *American Passenger Arrival Records — A Guide to the Records of Immigrants,* Genealogical Publishing Company. (1999)

10. USING THE LDS CHURCH

The Genealogical Society of Utah, affiliated with the Church of Jesus Christ of Latter-day Saints, is one of the premier genealogical organizations in the world. The Genealogical Society of Utah and the **LDS church** have been actively involved in collecting genealogical information for over 150 years. Working with foreign governments, they have been methodically and tirelessly microfilming countless governmental and church records throughout the world. Even as you read this, hundreds of volunteers are scattered across the globe microfilming records. At the time of this printing, records have been filmed in over 110 countries.

The good news is that this information is then archived, and is available to anyone with a willingness to search through their records for them - whether they are members of the LDS church or not. There are three important areas you need to learn about as you become familiar with this wonderful resource for research. Those three areas are:

•Family History Library
•Family History Centers
•FamilySearch™ website

Let's talk about each one of these resources:

The Family History Library
Nerve central for all this genealogical activity is in Salt Lake City, Utah in a large building known as the **Family History Library**. The library was founded in 1894 with the intent of assisting members of the LDS church with their family history research. Since that time, the library and its resources have been made available to all, regardless of their religious affiliation. The building that currently houses the library was built in 1985, and is located at 35 North West Temple in Salt Lake City (Tel. 801/240-2331). It is open Monday from 7:30am to 5:00pm, and Tuesday through Saturday from 7:30am to 10:00pm. It is closed on Sundays, January 1, July 4, Thanksgiving and December 24 and 25.

USING THE LDS CHURCH

The genealogical collection is housed on five floors (four of them open to the public). At 142,000 square feet, it is the largest library of its kind in existence. Lighting, humidity and temperature control in the library are designed to protect the precious genealogical records from deterioration.

And is it ever a busy place! Hundreds of volunteers and full- and part-time employees labor to assist an average of 2,000 visitors that come through its doors each day. There is no charge to enter the library or use its services, nor is there a need to call for reservations.

The library boasts a genealogical collection that makes the mouth of any genealogist water. It has over 2.4 million rolls of microfilmed genealogical records, and 742,000 microfiche. There are over 310,000 books in the library's collections, most of them family histories. Their genealogical collection grows - mostly through the efforts of volunteers – at the rate of nearly 50,000 rolls of microfilm annually. It is estimated that over *750 million* names are contained in these records. That's a lot of people, and many of your ancestors are likely to be contained in those records.

Genealogical records are available from the United States, Canada, Europe, the British Isles, Latin America, Asia and Africa. The vast majority of the collection contains information on individuals that died prior to 1920.

I have been to the Family History Library, and it is as impressive as it sounds. For a time, I was fortunate enough to live in Salt Lake City, and I worked just a few blocks from the Library. Often, I would arrange to take my morning break at 11:45am, my lunch at noon and my afternoon break at 1:00pm, giving me nearly an hour and a half to do research on a fairly regular basis. Good idea, right? Wrong...I had to stop that practice because I found that I was continually calling back to work and taking the afternoon off as vacation because I had found a lead I just had to follow up on. While my ancestors loved it, my wife was not too thrilled about the practice.

Volunteers and employees in the Family History Library are anxious to assist you in your research efforts, whether you are just beginning your search, or whether you have been doing it for many years. They have experts in a variety of areas, including various foreign countries. They can help you get started or continue to unravel a genealogical mystery that you have been wrestling with for years.

Once you arrive, you'll find a host of supporting resources available to you in addition to the vast genealogical collection. There are over 500 microfilm and microfiche readers, over 200 computers available for visitors' use, copy machines for books and for microfilm. There are even scanners available that allow you to transfer information you find on microfilm to a CD. Tables and chairs are spread throughout the facility to allow you to study various and sundry materials.

The Library regularly schedules a variety of classes, including orientation classes and classes that focus on specialized research techniques. Call ahead or visit www.familysearch.org to see when these classes are scheduled.

It is impossible to have all these genealogical records stored on-site. Although most are there, and many are available via computer, it is wise to contact the Family History Library about four weeks before you visit to arrange for records that might not be kept on-site. To learn what records are available before your visit, go to **www.familysearch.org** and select *Library* and then click on *Family History Library Catalog*.

I have had personal experiences of finding long lost relatives while researching within the walls of this Library, and many friends can tell stories of searches with happy endings as a result of visits to the Family History Library.

Getting Around Salt Lake City
If you are fortunate enough to travel to Salt Lake City to visit and spend time in the Family History Library, you will likely be befuddled by seemingly incomprehensible addresses in Salt Lake City. You'll encounter addresses like:

709 North 700 East
2392 East 4400 South
1332 West 7100 South

Confusing, right? Wrong - once you understand the format, you will never need a map to get around in Salt Lake City. And the format is logical and easy: the first number and direction represent the street address; the second number and direction are the name of the street. There – got it? No? Read on.

The key to unfolding the mystery of these addresses is the LDS Temple in downtown Salt Lake City. All addresses in Salt Lake City tell you their relative location to the temple. For example, the address 4684 West 3100 South tells you that the house or building is located 46.84 blocks west of the temple and is on 3100 South Street (which is 31 blocks south of the temple). Taking the addresses above, the first is 7.09 blocks north of the temple and is on 700 East Street; the next is 23.92 blocks east of the temple on 4400 South Street, and the last is 13.32 blocks west of the temple on 7100 South Street (which is 71 blocks south of the temple).

The addresses immediately around the temple have a slightly more conventional naming scheme, but they still center on the temple. For example, the address of the Family History Library is 35 North West Temple. That tells you that the Library is .35 blocks north of the temple, and on West Temple Street. West Temple Street is the street that runs along the west side of the temple – also known as 100 West.

Once you understand the format, you will never need a map when looking for an address in Salt Lake City (or in most Utah towns, for that matter). In recent years it has been fashionable to name streets more conventional names, like Cherry Lane, Elm Street, etc. When faced with an incomprehensible address like 3145 South Maple Avenue, simply ask for the numbered street name of Maple Avenue, and you'll be told something like 2950 West. So now you know that the address on Maple Avenue is 31.45 blocks south of the temple on 2950 West Street.

Family History Centers
Okay, so you don't live in the Rocky Mountain region of the United States, nor do you plan on going to Utah any time soon. Does that mean that you are out of luck, that all these fabulous records are simply tantalizingly outside your grasp? Fortunately for you and me, the answer is, "Of course not." The LDS Church has provided alternate access to all of their genealogical records via their **Family History Centers**.

Considered branches to the Family History Library in Salt Lake City, Family History Centers are located literally throughout the world. Each is staffed by local volunteers who are interested in helping you conduct research on your family.

As of this printing, there are over 4,000 Family History Centers spread throughout the world, operating in every state in the United States and in nearly 100 countries throughout the world. And they are heavily used – over 100,000 rolls of microfilm are circulated to Family History Centers *monthly* – over one million rolls per year!

To determine whether there are any Family History Centers near you (there almost certainly are), go to the LDS Church's website at www.familysearch.org. Under the heading Family History Library system, click on the *Find a Family History Center Near You* label and you will be directed to a page where you can enter the city and state or country where you live, and within seconds you will be advised of any Family History Centers near you.

The hours of operation at the Family History Centers vary from center to center. Since each center is staffed solely by volunteers, the hours are dependent on the volunteers' availability. Generally speaking, each FHC is open two or three days a week for anywhere from four to twelve hours on those days. The telephone numbers listed are generally for phones located within the Center; if you get no answer to your call, try at various times, especially in the evenings between 6:00pm and 9:00pm. Or you can merely stop by the address and if the center is not open, there is almost always a sign indicating the hours the Family History Center is open. To narrow your time search, it is important to know that Family History Centers are never open on Sundays or Mondays. If you do not have Internet access, call 800/346-6044 and representatives there will help identify the closest Family History Center to you.

Many of the records that are housed at the Family History Library are available to researchers at each Family History Center. If you identify a record you want to search, you may order it through your local Family History Center. For a small postage fee (as of this writing: $3.25 for microfilm and $.15 per microfiche page), you can order most of these records. Microfilm or microfiche will arrive within a week or two (usually) at your local Family History Center, and you will be notified of their arrival. You may then go to the Center to view the microfilm or microfiche. They will remain in your local Center for six weeks, giving you ample time to review them. If for some reason that is not enough time, then you can extend them for another six weeks.

Each Family History Center is also equipped with computers and Internet access so that you can access the many records available on CD as well as contact the LDS Church's genealogy website, www.familysearch.org.

Getting the Most Out of Your Local Family History Center
As wonderful as they are, Family History Centers will be much more useful if you follow some basic guidelines.

USING THE LDS CHURCH

Prepare
Before you go to your local Family History Center, prepare for your visit. Have an idea about what line of your family (or what individual) you want to search for. Gather all the information you possibly can about the person or line that you want to research. Know surnames, city, county and/or state where they lived, and approximate dates of birth. The more information you can bring with you, the higher your likelihood of succeeding in your search.

Call Ahead
Before you just show up at one of the Family History Centers near you, call the contact number and confirm the location and hours of operation. Because the Centers are staffed solely by volunteers, Center hours and days of operation may vary as volunteers come and go. The website might not have the latest information on hours of operation.

If you are not successful in reaching anyone at the telephone number listed on the website, don't give up. Contact one of the local congregations and they can put you in touch with someone who knows the times that the Family History Center in that area operates. You can get a telephone number for local congregations by looking in your local white or yellow pages under the Church of Jesus Christ of Latter-day Saints. Here's a hint: since all LDS church leaders serve on a voluntary basis, doing their church work around their regular 8:00am to 5:00pm jobs, the telephone numbers listed are often only answered on Sundays or weekday evenings, when these volunteer leaders are most likely to be at the church building.

Have Patience
Finally, have patience with those who staff these Centers. Few are professional genealogists; in fact, the vast majority are not. They are individuals like you, who have a great love of genealogy and family research and want to help others have successful research experiences.

Let me stress that these Centers are open to anyone – regardless of religious belief – who has an interest in doing genealogy. In fact, records of attendance at these Centers indicate that something on the order of 60% of those who use Family History Centers are not members of the Church of Jesus Christ of Latter-day Saints.

Share Your Success
As mentioned earlier in this chapter, the Genealogical Society of Utah and the LDS Church provides these wonderful resources for genealo-

gists the world over. They are constantly adding to their collection. And that is where you come in. If you have had success in identifying ancestors through any of the LDS sources (or through any source, for that matter), please share that information with the LDS Church. It will become a part of their genealogical collection, which will in turn be available to other researchers who may be working on the same lines as you.

I have been contacted by genealogists as far away as Scotland who have gotten my name from genealogical information I had provided to the LDS church. It resulted in a new friend half a world away, and the sharing of more genealogical information between us.

FamilySearch

The LDS Church has developed an extensive genealogy website (www.familysearch.org) and database that allows individuals to gain access to the genealogical resources that the LDS Church has gathered through the years. It is called **FamilySearch**. It includes genealogical records for millions of individuals, from birth, death and marriage information to military records, census data, family histories, and much, much more. Like all other genealogical resources provided by the LDS Church, FamilySearch is available to anyone, regardless of religious affiliation.

The FamilySearch website was launched on May 24, 1999. From Day 1 it has been immensely popular – and incredibly busy. It gets roughly 10 million hits *each day*. Through its first nine complete years of existence (at the time of this writing), it garnered over 15 *billion* hits. It has definitely positioned itself as one of the premier websites available to genealogists.

Here's how it works: As you make a request for information, FamilySearch combs its extensive records, searching for matches on the name you entered. Not only that, it even matches last names that are spelled differently but sound the same (More/Moore, Fisher/Fischer, Smith/Smythe, Meier/Meyer, etc.).

Matches on the surname (if it was a surname search) then have links to allow the researcher to learn more about the record. In most cases, a short description gives details about the information contained in the record. It may include information about dates and places of birth, parents, marriage and death information, as well as information about children.

USING THE LDS CHURCH

Records in FamilySearch are divided into three important areas:

• Ancestral File
• Family History Catalog
• International genealogical Index

Ancestral File
From 1979 to 1999, members of the Church of Jesus Christ of Latter-day Saints and other researchers have contributed genealogical information to the Ancestral File. The information is in family form, as submitters complete Family Group Sheets and pedigree charts for the file. The Ancestral File contains nearly 40 million names, almost all of which have been gathered into families. It's likely that out of 36 million names, at least one of your ancestors is hiding out there.

One nice feature of the Ancestral File is that the names and contact information of individuals who submitted the information are available, so that other genealogists can coordinate research with their fellow genealogists.

The Ancestral File is accessible either via the LDS Church's genealogy website (www.familysearch.org), or on CD at each Family History Center.

Family History Library Catalog
This catalog describes all the records that are available in the Family History Library's collection. It allows genealogists to locate such genealogical records as birth, marriage and death records, family histories, census records, church records, military records and much more. The records may be in book, microfiche or microfilm format, or may even be available as computer files. The Family History Library Catalog is available on the Internet, on compact disk and on microfiche.

International Genealogical Index
The International Genealogical Index (or IGI for short) is a computer file that contains the names of over 725 million people from throughout the world. The Internet version is adding new names weekly. The names were gleaned from vital, church, and other records of individuals who were born between the early 1500s and the early 1900s. Like the Family History Library catalog, the IGI is available on the Internet, on compact disk and on microfiche.

Other Resources
In addition to these databases, FamilySearch contains several other databases, including:

•US Social Security Death Index (a computer file that contains records of deaths reported to the United States Social Security Administration. Most records start in 1962, but the file does contain a few records of deaths that happened before that date).

•Pedigree Resource File (a rapidly growing, lineage-linked computer file that contains the genealogical information for millions of individuals, family relationships and birth, marriage, and death information for millions of people). Anyone wishing to share genealogical information in this file may submit their records via the FamilySearch website.

•Vital Records Indexes (a collection of computerized databases that contains birth, christening, and marriage records from selected countries around the world).

A Practical Lesson In Using FamilySearch
Okay – so maybe you are following along, or perhaps I lost you on one of the early turns I took in this chapter. Let's walk through a little research lesson using one of my ancestors to see how easy it is to use Family Search. In the second chapter of this book, I "introduced" you to members of my family, including my great-grandfather, Edgar Quillen. As you'll learn elsewhere in the book (the *Census Records* chapter), locating the actual birthplace and birthdate of this beloved ancestor of mine has been a bit of a challenge. So let's use him as an example.

First, go to the FamilySearch website: www.FamilySearch.org. Upon arrival, you'll see in the top left quadrant of the box a place to enter the name and other information that might be helpful in locating this person. In my case, I will enter my great-grandfather's name (Edgar Quillen), but for the sake of this example, I will not enter his parents' names, although I am given the opportunity to do so by clicking the Advanced Search link below the information boxes. I may also enter information about his birth, marriage or death, within a range of years:

+ or – 2 years
+ or – 5 years
+ or – 10 years
+ or – 20 years

USING THE LDS CHURCH

Since I know he was born sometime close to 1880, I enter 1880 with a date range of + or – 5 years. Even though I think he was born in Virginia, there is some doubt about that, so I leave that space blank. Since I am open to varied spellings for his name (you should be too!), I do not click the box that says *Use exact spelling*. Then I click *Search*. Once I do that, FamilySearch scours its millions of records looking for my great-grandfather. In less time than it took for you to read that last sentence, FamilySearch returned the following information:

You searched for:	Edgar Quillen	(refine search)
		Birth/Christening 1875 – 1885
		Exact spelling: off
	Matches:	All source: 4

Ancestral File

1. Edgar Estell QUILLEN Ancestral File
2. Gender: M, Birth / Christening 15 Jan 1881, Lee, Virginia

Matches – Ancestral File: 1

Matches: International Genealogical Index – North America

2. Edgar Estil QUILLEN - International Genealogical Index / NA
Gender: M, Birth: 15 Jan 1880 Lee, Virginia

3. Edger Oates QUILLIN - International Genealogical Index / NA
Gender: M, Birth: 31 May 1884 Abbeville, Henry, Alabama

Matches: International Genealogical Index/North America - 2

Pedigree Resource File
4. Edgar P. Quillian - Pedigree Resource File
Gender: M, Birth/Christening: abt 1877
Matches: Pedigree Resource File - 1

Reprinted by permission. Copyright ©2003 by Intellectual Reserve, Inc.

So, after checking its databases, FamilySearch returned four possible matches: one from the Ancestral File, two from the International Geneallogical Index, and one from the Pedigree Resource File. Upon seeing this information, I recall that my great grandfather's middle name

103

was Estil, and one of the matches is for an Edgar Estil Quillen. So I eliminate choices #3 and #4, since both of those have different middle names. I also note that the last names for these two individuals are spelled in a slightly different manner: Quillin and Quillian (more on that later!).

But what of choice #1 – Edgar Estell Quillen? That is pretty close to my great grandfather's name. Here's the information for persons #1 and #2 side-by-side:

Edgar Estell Quillen, born 15 January, 1881, Lee County, Virginia
Edgar Estil Quillen, born 15 January, 1880, Lee County Virginia

Now, while it is possible that these two fellows are different people, I suspect that they are one in the same, and one genealogist or the other (or both!) submitted the information with inaccurate data. But, I am reasonably certain they are both the right person. I click on Contestant # 1, and see the following:

Edgar Estell QUILLEN (AFN: 1J78-HD1)	Pedigree Family
Sex: M	

Event: Birth	15 Jan 1881
	Lee, Virginia

Parents:		
Father:	Jonathan Baldwin QUILLEN (AFN: 1J78-H6R)	Family
Mother:	Susan Susanah (AFN: 1J78-H70)	

37456662	Edgar Estell	QUILEN	1J78-HD1	M	0
Submitters:					

Reprinted by permission. Copyright ©2003 by Intellectual Reserve, Inc.

Remember that the Ancestral File is the depository of information submitted to the Family History Department of the LDS Church by genealogists on pedigree charts and Family Group sheets. Therefore, there is generally information available about family members in addition to the individual. Clicking on *Pedigree Family* (on the top right-hand side of the form) takes me to the pedigree chart for Edgar Estell Quillen.

USING THE LDS CHURCH

Clicking on *Family* on the right-hand side of the *Parents* section yields the family group sheet for Edgar Estell Quillen – information about his wife and children.

Finally, clicking on the *Details* icon of the *Submitter* section provides me with the name and address of the individual who submitted this information. This is immensely helpful, as it gives me the opportunity to contact her and get more information about Edgar Estell Quillen (where she got her information, any additional information on other family members, etc.).

Now, getting back to the search results for Edgar Quillen, you'll see that the information on Contestant #2 came from the International Genealogical Index. Clicking on his name yields the following information:

Edgar Estil QUILLEN Sex: M	
Event(s): Birth: 15 Jan 1880, Lee, Virginia Christening: Death: 06 May 1978 Burial:	
Parents: Father: Jonathan Baldwin QUILLEN Mother: Sarah BURKE	
Messages: Form submitted by a member of the LDS Church. The form lists the submitter's name and address and may include source information. The address may be outdated. Details vary. To find the form, you must know the batch and sheet number.	
Source Information Batch Number: 8918001 Sheet 54 Source Call Number: 1553473 Type: Film.	

Reprinted by permission. Copyright ©2003 by Intellectual Reserve, Inc.

This screen tells me that the information is contained on a microfilm, Source Call Number 1553473 (this is sort of like a Dewey Decimal Number for microfilms). I can take this information to my local Family

History Center and request that microfilm. The Family History Library will send it to the Center closest to me, and I will be able to tell where the information about my great grandfather came from.

Now, in this case, I happened to know a little about the person I was searching for – his name and approximate year of birth. But you're not always fortunate enough to have that kind of information. One way to get a name and an approximate date is to look for family histories or other records that might provide information about members of my family. For information like that, I'll go to the FamilySearch home page again, but this time I will click on *Library* and then on *Family History Library Catalog*. The on-line catalog will tell us all the genealogical resources available to us in the Family History Library. Once we have clicked Family History Library Catalog, we will be given six choices:

•Place Search
•Surname Search
•Author Search
•Subject Search
•Call Number Search
•Film/Fiche Search

Since I know the surname I am looking for, I should click *Surname Search*. Next, I enter Quillen in the window, and click on Search. Here is what was displayed:

Quillen

A Backward glance: Quillen

The Cullinan and Cullinane family genealogy Cullinan, Michael S. (Michael Stephen), 1965-. Quillen

Descendants of the Quillen family (Quillin) of the Delmarva Penninsula McCabe, Vernon W. Quillen Morrison - Moffitt, Smith - Quillen families, 1800-1972 Honeywell, Mary E. Quillen (Mary Eveline Quillen), 1899-. Quillen

The Quillen family, an Ohio branch Honeywell, Mary E. Quillen (Mary Eveline Quillen), 1899-. Quillen

The Quillins: an historical and general magazine Quillen, C. G. Quillen

continued on next page

Strong family of Virginia and other southern states Rolff, James Robert, 1939-. Quillen

Windmills west, a Lackey family history Lackey, Sue Shockley. Quillen

Woollen—Woolen family biographical and historical records : and genealogy of Edmond — Edward Woollen of Dorchester County, Maryland and Richard Woollen of Maryland Woolen, Edward A., 1916-. Quillen

Yonts family tree Yonts, Jerry (Jerry Wes), 1951-. Quillen

Reprinted by permission. Copyright ©2003 by Intellectual Reserve, Inc.

Scanning that list, I note the book *Strong Family of Virginia and Other Southern States*, by James Robert Rolff. I know that my great-grandfather's family lived in Virginia for many years. So this book is of interest to me, as it may shed some genealogical light on that side of my family. Therefore, I click on that book title, and see the following:

Title	View Film Notes Strong family of Virginia and Other Southern States
Stmnt.Resp.	by James Robert Rolff
Authors	Rolff, James Robert, 1939- (Main Author)
Notes	Partial bibliography: p. 431-432. Includes index. Includes Alley, Callahan, Colley, Quillen, Stanley, Weems and related families. John Strong (b.ca.1675) moved from Hanover County to New Kent County, Virginia during or before 1698. Descendants lived in Virginia, North Carolina, Georgia, Mississippi, Tennessee, Kentucky and elsewhere. Includes records of some early Strong residents of Virginia, without establishing lineage to John.
Subjects	Strong Alley Callahan

continued on next page

107

Subjects	Colley Stanley Quillen Weems

Copies	
Call Number	Location
929.273 St88r	JSMB US/CAN Book
Format	Books/Monographs (With Fiche)
Language	English
Publication	Oak Forest, Ill. : J.R. Rolff, 1982, c1983
Physical	487 p.
Subject Class	929.273 St88

Even though this book is primarily about another surname than Quillen (Strong), it does contain some reference to the Quillen surname. I click on the *View Film Notes* icon (at the top right) to learn more about the microform version of this book. Here is what I see:

Title	Strong family of Virginia and other southern states
Authors	Rolff, James Robert, 1939- (Main Author)
Note	Location Film
Also on microfiche. Salt Lake City :	FHL US/CAN Fiche
Filmed by the Genealogical Society of Utah, 1992. 6 microfiches; 11 x 15 cm.	6100949

Now I have all the information I need to order the microfiche (FHL US/ CAN Fiche 6100949) of this book that contains information about members of the Quillen family in Virginia. I can now take this information to my Family History Center and order the microfiche of the book. Within one or two weeks it will arrive, and I have six weeks to review the information contained therein.

Pretty easy, and I didn't even have to drive to Salt Lake City!

USING THE LDS CHURCH

The more you work with the resources of the Church of Jesus Christ of Latter-day Saints, the more you will learn what is available there. I have worked with their resources for years, and I still find things that I didn't know about. But for now, you are armed with the information you need to begin your genealogical research for your ancestors using the records of the LDS Church.

LDS Church Checklist

___ If you are able to go to Salt Lake City, Utah to go to the Family History Library, determine what information you are seeking before you go.

___ Before you go to Salt Lake City, gather all necessary genealogical information you may need while you are at the library.

___ Familiarize yourself with the genealogical services offered by the LDS Church

___ Understand the value of Family History Centers and how to get the most out of them.

___ Prepare the names you are doing research on before you go to a Family History Center.

___ Call your local Family History Center to determine days and hours they are open.

___ Be patient with Family History Center volunteers.

___ Locate the website for FamilySearch (www.familysearch.org).

___ Familiarize yourself with the information that is available on the FamilySearch website.

Additional Resources

Parker, J. Carlyle, *Going to Salt Lake City to Do Family History Research,* Marietta Publishing Company. (January 1996)

Warren, Paula Stewart and James W. Warren, *Your Guide to the Family History Center,* Betterway Publications. (August 2001)

Warren, Paula Stewart and James W. Warren, *Making the Most of Your Research Trip to Salt Lake City,* Warren Research and Publishing. (August 2001)

11. CENSUS RECORDS

Do you remember your best friend from elementary school? You know – the one you could tell your deepest, darkest secrets to? The one who you could tell anything? Your best friend was the one who knew everything about you. He or she was easy to get along with, and you always enjoyed their company.

Well, let me introduce you to what may well be a genealogist's best friend: the **United States Federal Population Census**. Like your best friend from days gone by, the census has secrets to reveal to you that will be some of the very best secrets you've ever known. But these secrets are about your forefathers. The information they will share is a great beginning to just about any genealogical research project. And, like your best friend in elementary school, they are easy to get along with and are easy to understand.

Who, What, When, Where, Why & How...
Perhaps you remember from your junior high or high school days the "5 Ws" of good journalism: telling the Who, What, When, Where, Why, and How of a given situation. That is exactly what the US Census does. The Constitution of the United States called for the enumeration (census) of all of its citizens beginning in 1790 and continuing every ten years after that. The earliest censuses were little more than tally marks of the population, gathered together under the head of a family. But as the years progressed, they evolved to the point that they gathered very discrete information about each family and each family member in the United States.

Following is how censuses addressed the 5 Ws:

Who. Censuses were concerned with finding out the names of every person who lived in a certain area at a certain time. The censuses between 1790 and 1840 listed heads of family only, with tallies of all other

110

CENSUS RECORDS

persons in the household by age and sex. Every census since that time has included the names and ages of each and every person living at that location at that time.

What. The earliest US censuses focused on counting people only. As time went by, Congress realized that census takers could glean enormous amounts of information about the population by asking just a few additional questions. From its beginnings as a tallying system, it grew to provide such information as:

•Names, ages and sex of each person enumerated
•Race
•Occupation
•Real estate information (value, owned or rented)
•Birthplace of the individual and his / her parents
•Literacy
•Relationship to the head of the household
•Marital status and how long they had been married
•Number of children born to a mother, and how many were living at the time of the census
•Years they were a US citizen
•Language spoken
•Whether they had attended school in the last year
•Military status
•Disabilities

Imagine what a gold mine a census can be as you begin your research! I like them because they often tell me more about the individuals than just their names (things like their birthplace, occupation, infirmities, etc.). There is another important benefit that should not be overlooked: a census also gathers individuals together into families.

When. Each census took the enumeration for a given date. For example, the 1910 census captured information about every individual who was living in a particular household on April 15, 1910. Even if the census taker (also called an enumerator) didn't come by the house until October 1910, the question would be asked about those living in the house on April 15 of that year. (So – babies born after that date – even if it was before the enumerator asked the question – will not be included in the census; conversely, individuals who died after that will be included on the census.) The date varied from census to census; sometimes it is on the census page, and other times you have to do a little digging to discover the date used for enumeration purposes.

United States censuses were taken in the US every ten years between 1790 and today. Due to privacy laws, the latest census available for the public to view is the 1930 census. (By law, individual records cannot be released to the public until 72 years after the census in which they were collected.) All censuses between 1790 and 1930 are available to view and search, except the 1890 census. Tragically, the vast majority of the 1890 Census was destroyed in a fire (or by the water that was used to put out the fire!). Due to the 72-year rule, the 1940 census will not be available to the public until 2012 (1940 + 72 years = 2012).

Where. Each census is very specific about where the people lived. The earliest censuses included the county and/or city where the family lived; later censuses included that information as well as the street addresses of the individuals. Each of the censuses from 1850 onward tell you where each individual was born, and each census beginning with 1880 also tells you where each individual's parents were born – wonderful, valuable genealogical information.

Why. As mentioned earlier, the initial reason for censuses was to determine legislative representation and for tax purposes. But Congress soon realized that important demographic information could be compiled from the census. Hence questions about national origin, literacy and occupation gave them a snapshot of what the nation looked like.

How. Enumerators went from house to house carrying large binders or tablets with the census template. They asked whoever was at home (presumably the oldest person available – preferably the head of the household) information about each of the individuals residing in the household on a given date. Just think of the difficulty that must have been in the days before ball-point pens! From the thousands of census pages I have looked at (all microfilmed), it appears that all enumerators were required to use pen and ink rather than pencil. Many is the time that I have imagined in my mind's eye a tired, dusty enumerator stopping at the way-out-in-the-middle-of-nowhere home of one of my ancestors and asking all those questions. (Thank you from the bottom of my heart, enumerators!)

Questions, Questions, Questions
As time went on, the census forms evolved, and additional questions that were of interest to the government were added. Following are the various questions that were asked for each census:

CENSUS RECORDS

1790
•Head of family
•Free White Males
    •16 and up, including head of family
    •Under 16
•Free white females
    •Including head
•All other persons
•Slaves
•County
•City

Note: No schedules are known to exist for the 1790 Census for Delaware, Georgia, Kentucky, New Jersey, Tennessee, and Virginia. It is thought that they were destroyed during the War of 1812 when the British attacked Washington. Some Virginia records are available from state enumeration records taken in 1790.

1800
•Head of family
•Free white males
    •Under 10
    •10 to 16
    •16 to 26
    •26 to 45
    •45 and over
•Free white females
    •Under 10
    •10 to 16
    •16 to 26
    •26 to 45
    •45 and over
•All others
•Slaves
•Remarks

1810
(Same as 1800)

1820
•Head of family
•Free white males
•Under 10

•10 to 16
•16 to 18
•16 to 26
•26 to 45
•45 and over
•Free white females
  •Under 10
  •10 to 16
  •16 to 18
  •16 to 26
  •26 to 45
  •45 and over
•Foreigners not naturalized
•Agriculture
•Commerce
•Manufacturers
•Free coloreds
•Slaves
•Remarks

1830
•Head of family
•Free white males
  •Under 5, 5 to 10, 10 to 15, 15 to 20, 20 to 30, 30 to 40, 40 to 50, 50 to 60, 60 to 70, 70 to 80, 80 to 90, 90 to 100, over 100
•Free white females
  •Under 5, 5 to 10, 10 to 15, 15 to 20, 20 to 30, 30 to 40, 40 to 50, 50 to 60, 60 to 70, 70 to 80, 80 to 90, 90 to 100, over 100
•Slaves
•Free colored

1840
(Same as 1830)

1850
•Name
•Age
•Sex
•Color
•Occupation
•Value of real estate
•Birthplace
•Married within year

•School within year
•Cannot read or write
•Enumeration date
•Remarks

1860
•Name
•Age
•Sex
•Color
•Occupation
•Value of real estate
•Value of personal property
•Birthplace
•Married in year
•School in year
•Cannot read or write
•Enumeration date
•Remarks

1870
•Name
•Age
•Sex
•Color
•Occupation
•Value of real estate
•Value of personal property
•Birthplace
•Father foreign born
•Mother foreign born
•Month born in census year
•School in census year
•Can't read or write
•Eligible to vote
•Date of enumeration

1880
•Name
•Color
•Sex
•Age June 1 in census year
•Relationship to head of house

•Single
•Married
•Widowed
•Divorced
•Married in census year
•Occupation
•Other information
•Can't read or write
•Place of birth
•Place of birth of father
•Place of birth of mother
•Enumeration date

1890
Note: the vast majority of the 1890 census was destroyed in a tragic fire. Only fragments remain.

1900
•Name of each person whose place of abode on June 1, 1900 was in this family
•Relation to head of family
•Sex
•Color
•Month of birth
•Year of birth
•Age
•Marital status
•Number of years married
•Mother of how many children
•Number of these children living
•Place of birth
•Place of birth of father
•Place of birth of mother
•Years of immigration to US
•Number of years in US
•Naturalization
•Occupation
•Number of months not employed
•Attended school (months)
•Can read
•Can write
•Can speak English
•Home owned or rented

•Home owned free or mortgaged
•Farm or house

1910
•Name of each person whose place of abode on April 15, 1910 was in this
    family
•Relation to head of family
•Sex
•Race
•Age
•Marital status
•Number of years married
•Mother of how many children
•Number of these children living
•Place of birth
•Place of birth of father
•Place of birth of mother
•Years of immigration to US
•Naturalized or alien
•Language spoken
•Occupation
•Nature of trade
•Employer, worker or own account
•Number of months not employed
•Can read and write
•Attending school
•Home owned or rented
•Home owned free or mortgaged
•Farm or house
•Civil War veteran
•Blind or deaf-mute

1920
•Name of each person whose place of abode on January 1, 1920 was in
    this family
•Relation to head of family
•Home owned or rented
•Home owned free or mortgaged
•Sex
•Color or race
•Age
•Marital status
•Years of immigration to US

•Naturalized or alien
•Year of naturalization
•Attending school
•Can read or write
•Place of birth
•Mother tongue
•Place of birth of father
•Mother tongue of father
•Place of birth of mother
•Mother tongue of mother
•Can speak English
•Occupation

1930
•Name of each person whose place of abode on April 1, 1930 was in this family
•Relationship of this person to the head of the family
•Home owned or rented
•Value of home, if owned, or monthly rental, if rented
•Radio set
•Does this family own a farm?
•Color or race
•Age at last birthday
•Marital condition
•Age at first marriage
•Attended school or college any time since Sept. 1, 1929
•Whether able to read or write
•Place of birth
•Place of birth of father
•Place of birth of mother
•Mother tongue (or native language) of foreign born
•Year of immigration into the United States
•Naturalization
•Whether able to speak English
•Trade, profession, or particular kind of work done
•Industry or business
•Class of worker
•Whether actually at work yesterday
•Whether a veteran of U.S. Military or naval forces
•What war or expedition
•Number of farm schedule

CENSUS RECORDS

Soundex

If you do genealogical work at all with the US Census, you will sooner or later (probably sooner) come across a term and tool called **Soundex**. Beginning with the 1880 Census, each of the censuses has been indexed – *sort of.* (Note: only twelve southern states were Soundexed for the 1930 US Census.) The index is not the typical alphabetical index you are familiar with. Rather, the Soundex indexing system attempts to provide all the advantages of an alphabetic index, yet at the same time tries to eliminate the vagaries of spelling variations for names. For example, if you were researching the name Cronin, in a strictly alphabetic index you might miss some ancestors who spelled their name *Kronin* or *Chronin.* Once you learn how to use the Soundex system (which you'll learn if you continue reading), I think you'll agree it is a remarkably ingenious way of indexing. I guarantee it will be worth your time to learn this ingenious method of indexing, as it will save you hours upon hours of reading census page after census page.

Each surname is assigned a four-digit alphanumeric code. The first letter of the individual's surname is always the first letter of the Soundex code. From that point, you ignore all vowels (A, E, I, O, and U) as well as the letters H, W and Y. Then, assign a numeric value to the next three consonants.

Soundex Coding Rules

Use the following coding scheme to determine the Soundex code for the names you are researching:

• 1 for the letters B, P, F, and V
• 2 for the letters C, S, K, G, J, Q, X and Z
• 3 for the letters D and T
• 4 for the letter L
• 5 for the letters M and N
• 6 for the letter R

Then follow these (relatively) easy Soundex rules:

1. Always use the first letter of the surname, regardless of whether it is a consonant or a vowel;
2. After the initial letter of a surname, ignore all vowels (A, E, I, O, and U) as well as the letters H, W and Y;
3. Double consonants (ll, nn, etc.) are counted as one letter;
4. Only code the first three consonants after the first letter of the name – ignore the remaining consonants;

5. If a surname does not have three consonants after the first letter of the name, the number 0 is used to fill in the rest of the code.
6. Side-by-side letters that have the same Soundex code should be counted as one letter. For example, ignore the K and S in Dickson, since C, K and S all have the same Soundex code. This applies to first and second letters in a surname also.
7. If a surname has a prefix (Van, D', Von, etc.), then code the name with and without the prefix – the indexer may have used either name for coding.

Let's do a few examples to get you used to the idea and to see how it all works:

The surname Hudson would be coded H-325:

•Ignoring the vowels, H, W, and Y, Hudson becomes *Hdsn*, and:
•H = the first letter of the surname
•3 = the numeric code for the letter D
•2 = the numeric code for the letter S
•5 – the numeric code for the letter N

Note that when considering the consonants in the rest of the name, we ignore any letter H (Rule #2), but since it is the first letter of the surname, we use it in the code.

The surname Quillen would be coded Q-450:

•Ignoring the vowels and the double ll (Rules #2 and #3), Quillen becomes Qln;
•Q = the first letter of the surname;
•4 = the numeric code for the letter L
•5 = the numeric code for the letter N
•0 = the numeric code when there are no other consonants (see Rule #5)

Now because of this simple system, I don't have to concern myself with whether the name in the census record was spelled Quillan, Quillen, Quillin, or Quillon. The Soundex code for each one is Q-450.

Let's try a longer name: the surname Techmeyer would be coded T-256:

•Ignoring the vowels, the H and the Y (Rule #2), Techmeyer becomes Tcmr;
•T = the first letter of the surname;

•2 = the numeric code for the letter C
•(We ignore the H – Rule #2)
•5 = the numeric code for the letter M
•6 = the numeric code for the letter R

The surname See would be coded S-000

•Ignoring the vowels, See becomes *S*;
•S = the first letter of the surname
•0 = the numeric code for no additional consonants (see Rule #5)
•0 = the numeric code for no additional consonants (see Rule #5)
•0 = the numeric code for no additional consonants (see Rule #5)

The surname Van Brederode could be coded V-516 or B-636 (see Rule #7):

•Ignoring the vowels (Rule #2), Van Brederode becomes Vnbrdrd;
•V = the first letter of the surname;
•5 = the numeric code for the letter N
•1 = the numeric code for the letter B
•6 = the numeric code for the letter R

And we ignore the remaining consonants in the name (Rule #4)

OR

•Ignoring the vowels (Rule #2) and assuming the name was indexed under Brederode, Van Brederode becomes Brdrd;
•B = the first letter of the surname;
•6 = the numeric code for the letter R
•3 = the numeric code for the letter D
•6 = the numeric code for the letter R

And we ignore the remaining consonant in the name (Rule #4).

Hopefully, you can begin to see the power and versatility of the Soundex system of indexing. It is not flawless, however. As seen in the above example of a word with a prefix, that can pose a problem. Native American names might also pose a problem: did the researcher assign a Soundex code for *Painted* or *Shirt* for Painted Shirt, *Sitting* or *Bull* for Sitting Bull, etc. In cases like that, just code the name both ways and search for each coding.

Once you have converted the surnames you are searching for into a Soundex code, it's time to take the next step: searching through the Soundex cards.

Soundex Cards

Armed with the Soundex code, you'll now search the Soundex rolls for a match. Indexers (WPA workers) used index cards for each name on the census, and these cards are now on one of over 2,300 microfilm rolls. Unless you want to search through every state and US territory, you need to have at least a general idea of where your ancestor lived at the time of the census you are searching. At a minimum, you'll need to know the state your ancestor is from.

Soundex cards are arranged by state, and alphabetically and numerically within each state. For example, the card for the Addams family (A-352) would follow the card for the Asher family (A-260), even though if we were indexing strictly alphabetically Addams would precede Asher.

Following is an image of a Soundex card:

YEAR: 1880 1900 1910 1920 (Circle Year) **SoundexCard**

Head of Family			E.D.	Sheet
COUNTY		LOCALITY: City, Town or Municipal District		
SOUNDEX CODE	NATURALIZED? Yes No	IMMIGRANT YEAR	NATURALIZED YEAR	
OTHER MEMBERS OF FAMILY				
NAME		RELATIONSHIP	AGE	BIRTHPLACE

Soundex index only exists for 1880, 1900, 1910 and 1920 Censuses

CENSUS RECORDS

While there is genealogical information on this card, you'll be tempted to stop here. But don't do that – you've come most of the way on your journey to discover your ancestor on the census, and your goal is just around the corner. In addition to the important genealogical information on the card (which helps you to determine whether or not this is the right person), you'll find (in the top right-hand corner of the card) the E.D. (Enumeration District), the census sheet, county and locality. These identification marks will enable you to go to the actual image of the census page wherein this family is listed. Also note the Soundex code in the left-center portion of the card.

Once you have found a card that seems to match the person or family you are searching for, examine it closely. If you are looking for your 2nd great grandfather and you think he was born around 1850, then the person listed on this card should have his name, an approximate age of 30 (if you are looking at a card for the 1880 census), and correct color and sex.

Note that there are only seven lines for family members on this card. Often, this won't be enough space to include all individuals living with the person listed. In those instances, another card will follow this one with the additional individuals on it. It will have the head of the family's name on it, along with the additional individuals, but it will not have the ED, volume, sheet, etc. listed.

If you believe this is the card for your ancestor, copy the information down.

The Census
Using the information from the card, you should be able to locate the exact place in the census where your ancestor is found. Once you find the correct state, search for the county that is listed on the Soundex card. (Note: If your ancestor lived in a large city, it may be listed separately from the county the city is in.) Counties are listed alphabetically, and along the left side is the information that indicates which microfilm number contains the census schedule for that area.

Obtain the microfilm roll, then using the microfilm reader, fast forward to the Enumeration District, sheet and volume number indicated on the Soundex card. Once you arrive at the page, look for the individual or family that is listed.

Write it Down!

Now that you've found your ancestor and his or her family, what next? First and foremost, write down the information exactly as it appears on the census. Writing the information down exactly is very important. For example, even though you KNOW that your great grandmother's name was *Susan,* if her name appears as *Susannah* on the census, resist the temptation to "correct" the entry when you copy the information. It may just be that the family traditions about her name being Susan are incorrect, and that her real name was Susannah.

I had an interesting experience with that in my own family. Family tradition held that my great grandmother was born in Arkansas. Yet when I located her as a child on a census schedule, it listed Texas as her state of birth. Even though I knew that wasn't right, I wrote the information down exactly as it appeared. Years later, I learned from one of my great aunts that my great grandmother's birth place really was Texas...she only told people she was born in Arkansas because she was embarrassed to admit she was born in Texas! (My apologies to those from the Lone Star state!)

Back to writing exactly what appears: write the information on a piece of paper. You can also go to the LDS Church website (www.familysearch.org) and copy any of the blank census templates that are available there. If you are lucky, the library where you are reviewing census records has a microfilm reader that also will make copies of the microfilm page you are viewing. This is the most accurate and efficient method of preserving the information. Often, a library that has 10 or 20 microfilm readers may only have one or two that can make copies. It is well worth your time to check with the librarian to see if they have a reader that makes copies, because if they do, it will save you a lot of time.

What Next?

Okay, so now you have found your great grandfather in the US Census. Now what do you do? Before you declare victory and move on – consider a caution. While the amount of information that is found in censuses is immense, remember that it is considered a secondary source of information – much of the information was written down many years after the event happened. Events like place of birth of parents, year and or months of birth, etc., could be incorrect. Consider the following *Census Conundrum* for my own great grandfather.

According to my great grandfather, Edgar Estil Quillen, he was born January 15, 1880 in Lee County, Virginia. He was the son of Jonathan

CENSUS RECORDS

Baldwin Quillen and Sarah Minerva (Burke) Quillen. Following is the critical information that several censuses contain about these individuals through the years:

1880 Census – enumerated June 1, 1880

Quillen, Jonathan B. Head of House, 35 years, born in Tennessee
Sarah M. Wife, 34 years old, born in Virginia
Emmett V. Son, 9 years old, born in Virginia
Thomas F. Son, 8 years old, born in Virginia
Lizzie L. Daughter, 3 years old, born in Virginia
William E. Son, 1 year old, born in Virginia

Here's my first conundrum. My great grandfather says he was born in Virginia in January 1880. Yet here is his family on June 1, 1880, and he is not listed with them, but he would have been, had he actually been born in 1880. Perhaps he was born after June 1, 1880, or on January 15, 1881.

1890 Census

Destroyed, so there was no information available for this family.

1900 Census – enumerated June 7, 1900

Quillen, Jonathan B. Head of House, born in May 1845, 55 years, born in Tennessee
Sarah M. Wife, born September 1846, 54 years old, born in Virginia
Lizzie L. Daughter, born April 1877, 23 years, born in Virginia
William E. Son, born February 1879, 21 years old, born in Virginia
Edgar E. Son, born October 1881, 18 years old, born in Virginia
Creed C. Son, born July 1882, 17 years old, born in Tennessee
Charles C. Son, born January 1885, 15 years old, born in Tennessee
Henry P. Son, born September 1889, 10 years old, born in Tennessee

Conundrum # 2 – this census shows my great grandfather's birth date as October 1881, not January 1880 as my great grandfather always said. But – that explains why he wasn't found on the 1880 census. So perhaps he wasn't born in 1880 after all.

1910 Census – enumerated May 10, 1910

Quillen, Edgar E. Head of House, 28 years old, born in Virginia
Dolly, Wife, 25 years old, born in Pennsylvania
Lee, son, 4 years old, born in Oklahoma
Helon, son, 3 years old, born in Oklahoma

The census says he is 28 years old on the day of enumeration (May 10, 1910). If that is true, then that would lend credence to the supposition that his birthday was probably October 1881. Had he been born in January of 1880 or 1881, the census would show his age as 30 (if he was born in 1880) or 29 (if he was born in 1881). But if he was born in October 1881, then he would have been 28 in May of 1910 – and he would have turned 29 in October 1910. Maybe we have it figured out. Let's see if the 1920 census supports that conclusion.

1920 Census – enumerated January 31, 1920
Quillen, Ed, Head of House, 39 years old, born in Tennessee
Dolly, wife, 35 years old, born in Pennsylvania
Lee, son, 15 years old, born in Oklahoma
Helon, son, 13 years old, born in Oklahoma
Lloyd, son, 9 years old, born in Oklahoma
Ruth, daughter, 6 years old, born in Oklahoma
Annabelle, daughter, 3 years, four months, born in Oklahoma

Okay, now this is getting a little silly. If he was born in October 1881, as we surmised from the last two censuses, then he should have been 38 on his last birthday, not 39. But if he was born in October 1880, then he would have been 39 on January 31, 1920. But that would have made the information from the last two censuses incorrect.

Just to cross us up a little bit more, his state of birth is now listed as Tennessee, not Virginia! This might explain why exhaustive searches of Virginia vital records have not turned up a birth record for him. His three younger brothers are also listed as having been born in Tennessee. Hmmm - maybe I should look in Tennessee for a birth record for him! Here is what the 1930 Census says about the Edgar Quillen family:

1930 Census – enumerated April 2, 1930
Quillen, Ed, Head of House, 48 years old at last birthday, born in Tennessee
Dollie, wife, 46 years old at last birthday, born in Pennsylvania
Lee, son, 25 years old at last birthday, born in Oklahoma
Ruth, daughter, 16 years old at last birthday, born in Oklahoma
Annabelle, daughter, 13 years at last birthday, four months, born in Oklahoma
Lois May, daughter, 8 years old at last birthday, born in Oklahoma

Well, the conundrum continues – had my great grandfather been born in October 1881, he would have been 48 at the time of this census, not 49.

It does however, support the Tennessee birthplace theory (or at least he - or whoever answered the enumerator's questions - thought that is where he was born!).

So what does all this tell us? For starters, it validates the difficulties of using only secondary sources. Secondary sources should be used as starting points to finding primary sources. They often provide wonderful clues (but sometimes those clues can be misleading!). I will continue my hunt for my great grandfather's birth certificate by looking in Tennessee in October 1881. These census reports have gotten me very close to this elusive ancestor of mine, but I really want to pin down the exact date of his birth by finding a primary source.

Secondly, it points out some of the foibles of the census process. As good as it is – and in my estimation it is very good – the census process is limited by the inaccuracies of humans providing information. Enumerators asked the oldest individual they could find at home for the information. In the case of my great grandfather, an older son may have been the only one available to answer questions, and he may have assumed his father was born in Tennessee and not Virginia, and he might also have made a mistake in estimating his father's age. I suppose the possibilities for error could go on and on.

Finding the Censuses
Notwithstanding the lack of exact information, I heartily recommend that you use census records to assist you in finding families you are searching for. So, where do you find them? There are several places. If you live in the state where your ancestors lived, the genealogy section of the state library will have at least your state's census records, and they may have the records for other states. (See Appendix B for a listing of state libraries nationwide.)

If the state library doesn't have the census microfilms, then there are fourteen locations of the national archives, and each has all the states' censuses on microfilm. The addresses, phone numbers, and websites for the centers are listed in chapter 8, *Genealogical Collections & Libraries*.

Hours vary from center to center. Generally, all offices are open Monday through Friday during normal business hours. Most offer at least one evening a week where they are open until 8:00pm and most are also open at least one if not two Saturdays per month. Before you go, call ahead or check each library's website for specific information about their hours of operation.

Finally, don't forget that your local Family History Center also allows you to order and view census microfilms from the Family History Library in Salt Lake City.

Mortality Schedules
Another important record that was kept coincident with the US Census was the Mortality Schedule for the 1850 through 1880 censuses. These schedules listed everyone who had died between June 1 of the year before the census and May 31 of the census year. They listed the name, age, sex, marital status, race, occupation, birthplace, cause of death and length of illness for each individual who passed away during that year. If you have an opportunity to search Mortality Schedules, you may find it interesting to note the ages of those who died. So many of them are children under age 10 - infant and young child mortality was very high in the mid-1800s. I guarantee it will tug at your heartstrings.

Census Records Checklist
____ Find the location of the nearest facility that has US Census records.

____ Determine which surnames you want to search for.

____ Determine the name of the head of household if not the ancestor you are looking for.

____ Know the approximate birth year of the ancestors you are searching for.

____ Try and discover the family's place of residence during the census year

____ Review the Soundex process, and develop the Soundex code for the ancestors you want to search for.

____ If possible, identify the names of siblings and parents of the ancestors you are searching for (this will help you identify the correct family).

____ Be sure and have pen and paper to record information found.

___ Obtain blank census templates to enter information you find (you can e-mail me and I'll send them to you).

Additional Resources

Carlberg, Nancy Ellen, *Beginning Census Research*, Carlberg Press (January 1992)

Dollarhide, William, *The Census Book: A Genealogist's Guide to Federal Census Facts, Schedules and Indexes*, Heritage Quest (1999)

12. MILITARY RECORDS

The information found in military records is an often-overlooked gold mine for genealogists. Information I have gleaned from pension records has enabled me to piece families together, and records of military service have made my ancestors seem like real people to me. And I suspect, with just a little effort on your part, you may have many of the same experiences. Read on and you'll get a few clues on how best to find your ancestors among the military records of our nation.

Motivation
The motivation for your ancestors' military service is as varied as the individuals who enlisted. It may have been for glory's sake, or to answer the call of their country to fight against oppression. It may have been a burning desire to abolish (or prolong) slavery, or merely to earn a paycheck and a roof (albeit canvas) over their heads during difficult economic times. Clearly, many American men have served in the military.

American Wars
In her storied history, Americans have fought in a number of wars. If you are not sure whether one of your ancestors fought, see if they were of military age (roughly 16 to 35) during any of these wars:

• French and Indian Wars (1754 to 1763)
• Revolutionary War (1775 to 1783)
• War of 1812 (1812 to 1815)
• Mexican War (1846 to 1848)
• Civil War (1861 to 1865)
• Spanish-American War (1898)
• Philippine War (1899 to 1902)
• World War I (1917 to 1918)
• World War II (1941 to 1945)
• Korean Conflict (1950 to 1953)
• Vietnam War (1965 to 1973)

MILITARY RECORDS

If they were of military age during any of those wars, it may well be worth your time to check out military records for genealogical information.

Where to Begin

First of all, decide what you want to know for whom. Perhaps your interest is in whether or not an ancestor served in the military, and if so, what battles he was engaged in. Or perhaps you really don't care about that, but would like to glean any genealogical information about that particular ancestor that might be included in military records.

When beginning your search, use common sense. If you are trying to find information from military records about an ancestor that was born in 1855, you probably won't find him listed in enlistment or service records for him during the Civil War! (However, you may find him mentioned in a pension application by his father or his widowed mother. More on that later.)

Let's use my third great grandfather as an example. Leonidas Horney was born in 1817. That would have made him the ripe old age of 44 at the time the Civil War broke out in 1861. Was he too old to participate in the Civil War? Perhaps. But it also put him at about the age of senior military officers. So, I might as well check Civil War military records to see if he may have served. Another possibility is that he may have served during the Mexican War. So I should check those records also.

In Leonidas' case, I had a bit of a clue, in that I have a picture of him in a Union Civil War uniform. I also knew that family tradition held that he had enlisted in Missouri. So as a shot in the dark, I got on the Internet and entered *Missouri Civil War Records*. I received 234,000 hits to my request and selected the first one: *Index to the Civil War in Missouri*. Once I got to the website, one of the options was *Index to Officers in Missouri Military Units*. I selected that, and within seconds had the following information:

Leonidas Horney, original commission: Captain, 10th Missouri Cavalry
Subsequent promotions:
Major 10th Missouri Cavalry
Lieutenant Colonel 10th Missouri Cavalry.

This was important information. While it might not look like genealogical information, it provides me an important element in researching military records – his military unit. Many US military records were kept by military unit.

The National Archives

At some point in your search for the military records of your ancestors, you will cross paths with the National Archives of the United States of America. The repository of all military records, the National Archives will likely yield you a great deal of genealogical information, if you only know (or learn) how to use them. The National Archives has the following military records available for research:

• Volunteer military service (1775 to 1902)
• US Army military records (1789 to 1917)
• US Navy records (1798 to 1902)
• US Marine Corps (1789 to 1904)
• US Coast Guard and its predecessors (Revenue Cutter, Life Saving Services, and Bureau of Lighthouses) (1791 to 1919)
• Civil War Service and pension records (Union as well as Confederate)

Here are the types of records available:

Enlistment Records

Enlistment records of soldiers can be very interesting. At a minimum, they will tell you the name, rank, date and place that the individual enlisted. They may also tell you such interesting tidbits as their occupation, age, physical description (height, weight, hair and eye color, complexion, size of hands and feet, etc.) and marital status.

Compiled Military Service Records (CMSR)

Every volunteer soldier has had compiled for him a Compiled Military Service Record (CMSR) for each regiment he served in. It contains basic information about his service career while in that regiment. Information contained within the record might be enlistment information, leave (vacation) requests, muster (roll call) records, and injury or illness reports. If he was killed in action, this will most likely be found in the record, or information about his discharge if he survived.

When I requested the service record for Colonel Leonidas Horney, my third great grandfather, I received documents that included the following:

• The date and place of his enlistment;
• His date of birth;
• His height, hair and eye color and color of complexion;
• The rank he enlisted as;
• The name of his regiment and company;
• The commanders he reported to;

•Several muster sheets showing his presence on specific dates (muster sheets are like roll calls);
•A copy of a letter from his commanding officer granting him a two-month leave;
•Several documents detailing his promotion from Captain to Major to Lieutenant Colonel;
•Two casualty sheets, one detailing a slight injury sustained at the Battle of Corinth and the other reporting his death in the Battle of Champion Hill, Mississippi on May 16, 1863.

Pension Records
Pensions were applied for by Union army soldiers, their widows and / or their minor children. Because of the need to ensure that the applicant was indeed related to the former soldier, a great deal of information was often requested to substantiate the relationship. A widow, for example, would have had to provide the date and place of their marriage (and often the name of the person who performed the marriage). She would often be required to provide either the marriage certificate, or a certified record signed by the minister who performed the ceremony. If the widow had children under the age of 16, she also needed to provide proof of their birth in the form of a birth certificate, or a government-certified document that provided the child's name, birth date and birth place – all genealogical nuggets.

Pension files are all indexed by the **National Archives and Records Administration** (NARA), and the index is available at National Archives locations or at the following website: www.archives.gov/research_room/genealogy/military/pension_index_1861_to_1934.html.

When I searched for the pension record for one of my ancestors who served in the military and fought in the Civil War, I found a plethora of information about him and his family. After his death, his widow completed a series of affidavits that contained the following information:

•Her full maiden name;
•Her age and birth date;
•Her birth place;
•The date and place she married her husband;
•The name of the person who performed their marriage ceremony;
•The names, birth dates and ages of all their children 16 years of age and younger;
•The names and birth dates of those children who had died.

That was truly a treasure trove of genealogical information.

Record of Events
Generally, not much of genealogical value is listed in the Records of Events. They are generally sort of journal entries that trace the movement of troops. Often, they are little more than places and dates that the various companies and regiments were stationed or marching to.

These would be of interest if you wanted to trace an ancestor's movements through the war. In the case of the Civil War, it would be interesting to see if any of your ancestors engaged in battles against one another. Numerous of my family lines lived in and around border states during the Civil War, and both the Confederate and Union armies had members of my family fighting for them.

Confederate Records
A special note about Confederate army records. Both Compiled Military Service Records (CMSR) and Records of Events were kept for Confederate units. They are often not as complete as Union records of the same type, as many Confederate records did not survive the war. Pensions were granted to Confederate veterans and their widows and minor children by the states of Alabama, Arkansas, Florida, Georgia, Kentucky, Louisiana, Mississippi, Missouri, North Carolina, Oklahoma, South Carolina, Tennessee, Texas, and Virginia. Note that it was the *states* who granted these pensions, not the federal government; those records are contained in the State Archives of the state where the veteran resided after the war, not in the National Archives.

As mentioned above, pension records can be a valuable source of genealogical information. Below is the location of the offices for each of the states that granted Confederate pensions, and a little about their collections:

Alabama Department of Archives and History
624 Washington Avenue
Montgomery, AL 36130-0100
Telephone: 334/242-4363
Website: www.archives.state.al.us/index.html

In 1867 Alabama began granting pensions to Confederate veterans who had lost arms or legs. In 1886 the State began granting pensions to veterans' widows. In 1891 the law was amended to grant pensions to indigent veterans or their widows.

Arkansas History Commission
1 Capitol Mall
Little Rock, AR 72201
Telephone: 501/682-6900
Website: www.state.ar.us/ahc/index.htm

In 1891 Arkansas began granting pensions to indigent Confederate veterans. In 1915 the State began granting pensions to their widows and mothers.

Florida State Archives
R. A. Gray Building
500 South Bronough Street
Tallahasse, FL 32399-0250
Telephone: 850/487-2073
Website: www.dlis.dos.state.fl.us/index_researchers.cfm

In 1885 Florida began granting pensions to Confederate veterans. In 1889 the State began granting pensions to their widows. A published index, which provides each veteran's pension number, is available in many libraries.

Georgia Department of Archives and History
5800 Jonesboro Road
Morrow, GA 30260
Telephone: 678/364-3700
Website: www.sos.state.ga.us/archives/

In 1870 Georgia began granting pensions to soldiers with artificial limbs. In 1879 the State began granting pensions to other disabled Confederate veterans or their widows who then resided in Georgia. By 1894 eligible disabilities had been expanded to include old age and poverty.

Kentucky Department of Libraries and Archives
Research Room
300 Coffee Tree Road
Frankfort, KY 40601
Telephone: 502/564-8704
Website: www.kdla.ky.gov

In 1912, Kentucky began granting pensions to Confederate veterans or their widows. The records are on microfilm.

135

Louisiana State Archives
3851 Essen Lane
Baton Rouge, LA 70809-2137
Telephone: 504/922-1208
Website: www.sos.louisiana.gov/tabid/53/Default.aspx

In 1898 Louisiana began granting pensions to indigent Confederate veterans or their widows.

Mississippi Department of Archives and History
PO Box 571
Jackson, MS 39205
Telephone: 601/359-6876
Website: www.mdah.state.ms.us/

In 1888 Mississippi began granting pensions to indigent Confederate veterans or their widows.

Missouri State Archives
600 W. Main
PO Box 1747
Jefferson City, MO 65102
Telephone: 573/751-3280
Website: www.sos.mo.gov/archives/

In 1911 Missouri began granting pensions to indigent Confederate veterans only; none were granted to widows. Missouri also had a home for disabled Confederate veterans. The pension and veterans' home applications are interfiled and arranged alphabetically. Typically, the pension file is small, perhaps four to eight pages, containing a standard application form and may include letters of recommendation from family members or others.

North Carolina State Archives
Physical address:
109 East Jones Street
Raleigh, NC 27601-2807
Telephone: 919/733-7305
Website: www.ah.dcr.state.nc.us/archives/

Mailing Address:
4614 Mail Service Center
Raleigh, NC 27699-4614

MILITARY RECORDS

In 1867 North Carolina began granting pensions to Confederate veterans who were blinded or lost an arm or leg during their service. In 1885 the State began granting pensions to all other disabled indigent Confederate veterans or widows.

Oklahoma Department of Libraries, Archives and Records Management Division
200 Northeast 18th Street
Oklahoma City, OK 73105
Telephone: 800/522-8116 (nationwide) ext. 209
Website: www.odl.state.ok.us

In 1915 Oklahoma began granting pensions to Confederate veterans or their widows.

South Carolina Department of Archives and History
8301 Parkland Road
Columbia, SC 29223
Telephone: 803/896-6100
Website: www.state.sc.us/scdah

A state law enacted December 24, 1887, permitted financially needy Confederate veterans and widows to apply for a pension; however, few applications survive from the 1888-1918 era. Beginning in 1889, the SC Comptroller began publishing lists of such veterans receiving pensions in his *Annual Report*. From 1919 to 1925, South Carolina granted pensions to Confederate veterans and widows regardless of financial need. These files are arranged alphabetically. Pension application files are typically one sheet of paper with writing on both sides. Also available are Confederate Home applications and inmate records for veterans (1909-1957), and applications of wives, widows, sisters, and daughters (1925-1955).

Tennessee State Library and Archives
Public Service Division
403 Seventh Avenue North
Nashville, TN 37243-0312
Telephone: 615/741-2764
Website: www.tennessee.gov/tsla/

In 1891 Tennessee began granting pensions to indigent Confederate veterans. In 1905 the State began granting pensions to their widows. The records are on microfilm.

Texas State Library and Archives Commission
PO Box 12927
Austin, TX 78711
Telephone: 512/463-5480
Website: www.tsl.state.tx.us/index.html (Main website)
Website: www.tsl.state.tx.us/arc/genfirst.html (Genealogy)
Website: www.tsl.state.tx.us/arc/index.html (Archives and Manuscripts)

In 1881 Texas set aside 1,280 acres for disabled Confederate veterans. In 1889 the State began granting pensions to indigent Confederate veterans and their widows. Muster rolls of State militia in Confederate service are also available.

Library of Virginia
Archives Division
800 East Broad Street
Richmond, VA 23219
Telephone: 804/692-3888
Website: www.lva.lib.va.us/

In 1888 Virginia began granting pensions to Confederate veterans or their widows. The records are on microfilm.

Bounty Land Warrants
The Continental Congress discovered a way to pay its veterans or their widowed and orphaned dependents by giving them cash or (preferably) public lands. Laws passed between 1776 and 1855 authorized granting warrants for land to those who had served in the Revolutionary War, the War of 1812, the Indian Wars and the Mexican War.

The documents in a Bounty Land Warrant file are similar to those contained in pension files. They are particularly rich in genealogical data if it is the widow or children of the veteran who applied for the Bounty Land Warrant.

Other Resources
As you begin to plow the fertile ground of military records in search of your ancestors, understand that that there are far more records available than I can possibly list in this book. Veterans' census records, indexes to old soldiers' homes, indexes for soldiers' cemeteries, and Veterans' societies are just a few of the other resources that are available. The Church of Jesus Christ of Latter-day Saints has published a research outline for military records that gives an excellent overview of the records

138

MILITARY RECORDS

that are available to researchers: *US Military Records – Research Outline,* Intellectual Reserve, Inc. It is available through the LDS Church Distribution Center in Salt Lake City, Utah (Tel. 800/537-5950) for a small fee.

Okay – So Where Do I Find These Wonderful Records?
While some of the records we have been discussing have been micro-filmed, most have not. Your first stop should be to either a regional National Archives site (see the list at the end of Chapter 8 on *Libraries*), or perhaps to your local LDS Family History Center. They will have indexes that will help you determine whether or not your ancestor's records are part of those that have been microfilmed or not. If they have been microfilmed, then you may be able to view them at the location you are at.

In all probability, however, you will not be able to view the records at the regional National Archives center you are at or even at the Family History Center. You have several options. The first option is to visit the National Archives site in Washington DC. If that is not practical or possible – don't fret – you may write and request photocopies of the records. You'll need to obtain a number of copies of the National Archives Trust Fund (NATF) Form 85 for Pensions and Bounty Land Warrants and Form 86 for Military Service Records. These forms are available for free upon request. You may order the forms by writing to:

National Archives and Records Administration
Attn: NWCTB
700 Pennsylvania Avenue, NW
Washington, DC 20408-0001
Website: www.archives.gov/global_pages/inquire_form.html#part_a.

Each form (one per soldier or sailor) should be filled out with as much information as you have on the individual, but at least with his complete name, the war he fought in, and the state where he enlisted. If you know his regiment or company, include that also. The form should then be submitted to the National Archives address above.

Because federal law requires all such requests for information to be accompanied by a signature, forms must either be mailed or faxed.

The National Archives personnel simply do not have the time available to conduct extensive research for individuals, and for that reason it is important to provide as much information about the soldier as you can, so that they can determine without error that they have found the right soldier and records. If the request isn't clear enough, they may reject the request, asking for more information, or they may copy all the records of the soldiers they think might fit the request you sent.

The Internet and Military Records
I know there is an entire chapter on doing genealogy on the Internet in this book. But I felt like it was still worth giving a special mention in this chapter. The advent of the Internet has increased access to (and knowledge of!) a multitude of resources, including military records. I began scouring military records in the late 1970s and early 1980s – prior to the general proliferation of the Internet. In those days, the process was:

Request a form via mail.
Wait.

Complete and mail the form.
Wait.

Receive a rejection.
Sigh.

Complete another form and mail it.
Wait.

But the Internet has collapsed the above weeks- or months-long process to a matter of moments in many cases. The example I used earlier in the chapter about Leonidas Horney is a good example of the consolidated timelines the Internet provides. I had performed that search in the 1980s for him. At that time, it took around five weeks to get the same information that I received within literally 30 or 40 seconds on the Internet. That's powerful!

Military Records Search Checklist
____ Identify an ancestor you think may have served in the military.

____ Decide what you want to learn.

____ Understand what military records are available to research.

____ Determine (if possible) the branch of service in which your ancestor served.

MILITARY RECORDS

___ Understand the process for obtaining records (Internet, mail request, personal visit).

___ Select a record to search.

___ Request Form 85 or 86, complete and mail to the National Archives for your ancestor.

Additional Resources

Beers, Henry Putney, *The Confederacy: A Guide to the Archives of the Confederate States of America*, Smithsonian Institution Press, (August 1986)

General Index to Pension Files 1861–1934, National Archives and Records Administration Microfilm Publication T288.

Hewett, Janet B., editor, *The Roster of Union Soldiers, 1861 – 1865*, 33 volumes. Wilmington, North Carolina, Broadfoot Publishing, 1997.

Intellectual Reserve, Inc., *US Military Records – Research Outline* (a publication of the Church of Jesus Christ of Latter-day Saints)

Johnson, Richard S., *How to Locate Anyone Who is or Has Been in the Military*, 7th edition, Fort Sam Houston, Texas: Military Information Enterprises, 1996.

Military Service Records in the National Archives of the United States, National Archives and Records Administration (pamphlet produced by the NARA).

US War Department, *The War of Rebellion: A Compilation of the Official Records of the Union and Confederate Armies,* reprint: Gettysburg, Pennsylvania, The National Historical Society.

13. ETHNIC RESEARCH

America is the great melting pot where people of all nations have emigrated. In the stew of her population are a seemingly limitless number of ethnic groups, and individuals within those groups that are interested in tracing their ancestors. Massive efforts to microfilm records from all over the world have made previously unavailable documents available at the click of a mouse through the power of the Internet. Individuals no longer need to expend the time or money to travel to the lands of their ancestors' nativity to conduct their research.

AFRICAN-AMERICAN RESEARCH

In recent years, great strides have been made in the area of African-American research. One of the quintessential books on the topic was written by Dee Parmer Woodtor. It is called *Finding a Place Called Home: A Guide to African-American Genealogy and Historical Identity*, and it is an excellent resource for genealogists of African-American roots.

The search for ancestors after about 1870 is basically the same for African-Americans as it is for other ethnic groups. First of all, start with your parents, grandparents and if you're lucky enough - your great grandparents. Get the facts - when and where they were born and married, the names of their parents and siblings and vital information on each of them. Don't forget to visit with your aunts and uncles too to verify this information, or to find and hopefully resolve areas of discrepancy. Also, look for clues - and write them down - that might shed light on your pre-1870 family history.

Family traditions are important, but be willing to take them for what they are - clues to finding very small needles in very large haystacks. If the family tradition is that your 2nd great grandfather was a slave on a plantation in Mississippi and that he ran away and was caught and returned several times, consider it helpful to your research, but not necessarily the gospel truth. Generally speaking, even in stories that

142

may have been most embellished by dimming memories through the years, there is often a kernel of truth in them. Maybe your 2nd great grandpa didn't run away three times, but perhaps he did run away once. And that clue might be just the one you need to identify this ancestor in an era when accurate and specific records weren't kept.

It seems to me that successful researchers of African-American ancestry before 1870 need to have a higher degree of "detectivism" than other genealogists. All genealogists seem to possess a bit of this attribute, but it needs to be higher in researchers of African-American roots. America was not as good about keeping vital statistics (census, immigration, birth, death and marriage records, for example) on slaves. So that requires a little more creativity, a little deeper digging in non-traditional genealogical resources. And sometimes a combination of records needs to be researched and compared:

• 1850 and 1860 slave schedules
• Census records
• Civil War enlistment records
• Deeds
• Family Bible records
• Family histories and traditions
• Freedmen's Bureau records
• Letters
• Obituaries
• Old newspapers
• Plantation records
• Probate records
• Wills

Don't forget obituaries in your search for these elusive ancestors (actually, it's not the ancestors that are elusive, it's their records). True - the original records of the individuals being sought may be sketchy - if in existence at all. However, an obituary might shed immense light on your research. An ancestor born in 1850 who died at age 75 in 1925 may have important information revealed in his or her obituary. Perhaps it tells where and when he was born, names of children and/or parents and the name of his wife. It may reveal the state - or states - of the plantations where he was held in slavery. While obituaries are considered secondary genealogical resources, they may also be the only sources available, or perhaps may lead you to the location of other records that might be checked.

The obituary may help you pinpoint a place to search, and maybe even a timeframe. From there you can check local slave records, the appropriate slave schedules and perhaps even records of the plantation owner.

You may scratch your head about the suggestion to search Civil War enlistment records, but several hundred thousand slaves enlisted in the northern army. Records of these individuals were kept that may shed light on an ancestor or two.

In addition to Ms. Woodtor's book mentioned at the beginning of this section, there are several other excellent books on African-American genealogy. Look for *Black Roots: A Beginners Guide to Tracing the African-American Family Tree* by Tony Burroughs (Fireside Books) and *How to Trace Your African-American Roots: Discovering Your Unique History* by Barbara Thompson Howell (Citadel Printing). Both are excellent resources to help you begin searching for your African-American ancestors.

As mentioned earlier in this book, I have found genealogical societies to be immense helps to me in my personal research, and you may find that to be the case for your research. There are several genealogical societies dedicated to assisting in the search for African-American roots. Among the most active are:

Afro-American Historical and Genealogical Society, Inc.
PO Box 73067
Washington, D.C. 20056-3067
Website: www.aahgs.org/

The Afro-American Historical and Genealogical Society, Inc. is a nonprofit organization dedicated to preserving the history of African-Americans. They encourage active participation in genealogy and recording your findings so that others may benefit from your work. Membership in the organization is $35 for an individual or $40 for a family, and includes copies of the semi-annual *Journal of the Afro-American Historical and Genealogical Society* and the bi-monthly AAHGS News.

As of this writing, local chapters exist in 19 of the 50 states. Perhaps you would be interested in forming a local chapter if your state isn't currently represented. If so, the website lists its officers under the Organization tab, and there are several officers who serve as Chapter Establishment members.

ETHNIC RESEARCH

African-American Genealogy Group
PO Box 1798
Philadelphia, PA 19105-1798

While primarily focused on individuals who live in the Philadelphia area, the African-American Genealogy Group is nonetheless a valuable resource for those searching their African-American roots. Membership in the organization is $25 annually, and includes a subscription to their quarterly newsletter. A section of their website is dedicated for members to share their research in 17 southern and eastern states, including Alabama, Delaware, Florida, Georgia, Kentucky, Louisiana, Maryland, Mississippi, New Jersey, New York, North Carolina, Pennsylvania, South Carolina, Tennessee, Virginia, Washington DC and West Virginia.

The Schomburg Center for Research in Black Culture
515 Malcolm X Boulevard
New York, NY 10037-1801
www.nypl.org/research/sc/sc.html

The Schomburg Center for Research in Black Culture is devoted to collecting, preserving, and providing access to resources documenting the experiences of peoples of African descent throughout the world. Much broader than just a genealogical site, it nonetheless can be a source of assistance to African-American researchers.

Here are a few websites that you should peruse in your quest to find your African-American ancestors:

The **AfriGeneas** website can be found at www.afrigeneas.com. The home page of the website declares its purpose as: "...devoted to African-American genealogy, to researching African ancestry in the Americas in particular and to genealogical research and resources in general. It is also an African Ancestry research community featuring the AfriGeneas mail list, the AfriGeneas message boards and daily and weekly genealogy chats..."

The **Afro-Louisiana History and Genealogy** website can be found at www.ibiblio.org/laslave. Among other things, it provides a searchable database which contains background on 100,000 slaves who were brought to Louisiana in the 18th and 19th centuries. So if your roots go back to Louisiana, this is a website you definitely want to check out.

AOL has a Genealogy Forum website - www.genealogyforum.com - that is helpful to those researching their African-American roots. From the home page, click on any of several topics, and you'll be taken to a link that may be of use to you. Click on the Messages icon and you'll be taken to a message board where individuals are posting information about various individuals. Perhaps you'll find one of your ancestors hiding there. Under the same icon, look for Ethnic Resources, and click on African-American Resources, and you'll be whisked to a host of new websites specializing in African-American research.

African-American Military History
Website: www.lwfaam.net/

This site is dedicated to researching the military history and records of African-Americans involved in American wars. It provides resources and information about the significant role African-American troops have played through various conflicts.

Free African-Americans North Carolina, South Carolina, Maryland and Virginia
Website: www.freeafricanamericans.com/

This great website features a number of items, including excerpts from wills where owners who lived in North Carolina and Virginia freed their former slaves. It also includes tax roles, censuses and court records. In recent months, FamilySeach.org has added new collections of African-American research information, links and tools. They have developed a research tool called Quick Guide to African American Records. Another tool is called Finding Records of Your Ancestors, African Americans from 1870 to Present. Both tools are full of helpful hints and tips on how to begin and further your search for your African American ancestors. Both documents are available from the FamilySearch.org website in pdf format, and can be printed or viewed on-line.

NATIVE AMERICAN RESEARCH
Another tough area of genealogy is that of searching for your Native American roots. As with African-American genealogy, once you get back past the 1870s it becomes increasingly more difficult to do research in this area.

Prior to that time, the research process is pretty much the same as that for individuals researching other ethnic roots: start with what you know, expand that to what your parents and grandparents and other relatives know, and work your way back in history. Gather all the documentary evidence you can: birth and death certificates, marriage certificates, etc. In addition to being important primary sources, they may shed light on areas that you thought you had no information. They may identify a relative or birthplace that was heretofore unknown to you.

When researching Native American roots, knowing the tribal affiliation of your ancestors is critical. This will be a key element in your search.

If you can identify an ancestor who was living at the turn of the 20th century, you are in luck. Because if they were enumerated by census takers in the 1900 or 1910 Census, an additional page of information was completed for all Native Americans. Included were questions that identified the following:

• Other name (Indian name) of this Indian
• Tribe of this Indian
• Tribe of the father of this Indian
• Tribe of the mother of this Indian
• Has this Indian any white blood? (The 1910 Census asked for percentage of white, Indian and Black blood)
• Is this Indian, if married, living in polygamy?
• Was this Indian living on their own land? (1910 only)
• The type of dwelling this Indian is living in (civilized or aboriginal dwelling?)
• Graduated from which educational institution (1910 only)

These questions were included in a section of the census called Special Inquiries Relating to Indians. Answers to any of these questions will provide you with yet another piece of information to continue your search.

Another great source for Native American genealogical research are the **Dawes Rolls**. Henry Dawes was a US Senator who was appointed Commissioner of Indian Affairs. On February 8, 1887, the Dawes Act was passed by Congress and provided for the allotment of land to Native Americans of the Five Civilized Tribes living in Indian Territory (Oklahoma and Texas) on the following basis:

• To each head of a family, one quarter of a section (160 acres)
• To each single person over eighteen years of age, one-eighth of a section (80 acres)
• To each orphan child over eighteen years of age, one-eighth of a section (80 acres)

• To each living child under the age of eighteen, one-sixteenth of a section (40 acres)

The enrollment process took place between 1898 and 1906. The census was for people of the Cherokee, Choctaw, Chickasaw, Creek and Seminole tribes. Individuals were placed into the following categories:

• Citizens by blood
• Citizens by marriage (usually whites; the code used to identify these individuals was IW - meaning "intermarried whites")
• New born citizens by blood
• Minor citizens by blood
• Freedmen (former slaves of the Indians who were adopted into the tribes)
• New born freedmen
• Minor freedmen

The Dawes Act was viewed with suspicion by many Native Americans at the time of its passage. They were concerned that it was an elaborate method to identify and then relocate them (again). Nevertheless, many ventured forth and signed up. Many did not (can you blame them?).

Controversial or not, the Dawes Rolls provide 634 pages of double-columned, single-space typed list that provides the names, sex, age, tribal affiliation and percent of Indian blood for each individual. There are a number of websites where you can learn more about the Dawes Act and learn how to order copies of the allotment schedules. At the time of this writing, they could be purchased for as little as $25. One very informative website is **www.netmodem.com/dawes**. They are also available to view on microfilm at your local Family History Center. (Remember, the LDS Church charges only a minor shipping and handling cost to have microfilms delivered to local Family History Centers where they can be viewed for six weeks.)

Another enrollment effort for the Native Americans living in Indian Territory in the late 1800s and early 1900s was the **Guion Miller Roll**. Focused exclusively on the Cherokee tribe, the rolls contain important genealogical information. Growing out of one of the darkest chapters of US history, the Guion Miller Roll lists the names of Cherokees who were descendants of the individuals who participated in the 1835-1836 Trail of Tears – the forced relocation of the Cherokee Nation. Applicants needed to establish a link between them and those who were relocated. Over 45,000 applications were filed, listing over 90,000 individuals, so this is a rich source indeed. Information about the Guion Miller Roll can be found on several websites, one of the most informative being www.rootsweb.com/~cherokee/miller.html.

The index for the Guion Miller Roll can be accessed at www.archives.gov/ research_room/arc/arc_info/native_americans_guion_miller_index.html. If you find the names of an ancestor (or ancestors), you may order a copy of their application. The applications are contained on nearly 350 rolls of microfilm, and each application contains a great deal of genealogical information. Remember, individuals trying to prove their descent from those who walked the Trail of Tears must have demonstrated their familial connection to them. You should therefore be able to move at least two or three generations further along your family tree through these efforts.

There are several sources where you can order copies of applications. Again, your local LDS Family History Center is one source. Another is **The Indian Territory Genealogical and Historical Society**, c/o John Vaughn Library NSU, Tahlequah, Oklahoma 74464. To get a copy of the application from the ITGHS, send $5.00 and include a large, self-addressed and stamped envelope with your request. Your request should list the name of the applicant and his/her application number.

Cherokee Connections (Genealogical Publishing Company) by Myra Vanderpool Gormley is an excellent resource for those of Cherokee descent. It is focused on assisting individuals to establish their heritage for tribal membership. A side benefit is that it is a great book for those who are merely looking to extend that which they know about their lineage. It provides more details on the Dawes and Guion Miller Rolls, and points out other sources of research.

Another well-written and excellent resource is Bob Blankenship's Cherokee Roots (Cherokee Roots Publishing). Mr. Blankenship covers the US Censuses of the Cherokee Nation between 1817 and 1924. A two-volume set, the first volume covers those who lived east of the Mississippi River, and the second volume covers those members of the Cherokee tribe who lived west of the river.

AOL has a Genealogy Forum website - www.genealogyforum.com - that is helpful to those researching their Native American roots. From the home page, click on any of several topics, and you'll be taken to a link that may be of use to you. Click on the Messages icon and you'll be taken to a message board where individuals are posting information about various individuals. Perhaps you'll find one of your ancestors hiding there. Under the same icon, look for Ethnic Resources, and click on Native American Resources, and you'll be whisked to a host of new websites specializing in Native American research.

GERMAN RESEARCH

Willkommen! If your genealogical roots return to Germany, you are in good company. According to the 2000 US Census, 42 million people in America said they were of German ancestry – that's nearly one in six Americans.

Fortunately, the Germans were and are a hard-working, organized people. Their drive for orderliness will assist in your search for your German ancestors, as they created and kept many records. Unfortunately, two terrible World Wars fought on German soil also resulted in the loss of many of those records. Thankfully, many records survived despite the terrible destruction that accompanied those wars.

With more and more records being introduced onto the Internet, much of the research can be done from the comfort of your own home, or at least from the comfort of your own community.

Where to Begin?

As with any genealogical research, begin with yourself. What information do you already know? Perhaps you know a surname or two, and perhaps even the specific part of Germany where your line of the family came from (that is good!). As you begin searching, try to answer as many of the following questions as you can:

• Surname(s) of the individual(s) you are researching
• Names of parents, siblings, spouses (including maiden names of women), etc.
• County where they came from
• City or town they lived in
• Approximate years of critical events such as birth, death, marriage, etc.

Once you have gathered that information you are ready to further your search. Knowing something of Germany and its geographical structures is helpful. Germany is made up of many former and ancient kingdoms, provinces and duchies. Many of the records that were created are kept in the equivalent of the county seat of these various entities. There are sixteen states in Germany, and each is state is divided into counties. The German states are:

ETHNIC RESEARCH

Baden-Württemberg
Bayern (Bavaria)
Berlin
Brandenburg
Bremen
Hessen
Hamburg
Mecklenburg-Vorpommern

Niedersachsen
Nordhein-Wesphalen
Rheinland-Pfalz
Saarland
Sachsen
Sachsen-Anhalt
Schleswig-Holstein
Thüringen

Watch for these places when you are doing your research. While many may look foreign to you the first time or two that you see them, they may hold important genealogical keys.

One of the most important pieces of information for you to find while doing German research is the place where your ancestors came from. Once you identify the town, you can find that town on a map of Germany. A good gazetteer of Germany may be necessary to assist you in pinpointing which county (*kreis*) the town is in, which in turn will indicate what state it is in. Many German records are kept at the city, county and state levels.

And how do you find those places where your ancestors came from? Well, there are a number of ways. One of the best is the **Hamburg Passenger Lists**. The Hamburg passenger lists are a treasure trove of information containing the names of several million Europeans who came to America through the port of Hamburg between 1850 and 1934 (few records were kept during the years of World War I, 1915 - 1919). The emigrants were predominantly Germans.

The passenger lists may be just what you need to locate the town from which your ancestor emigrated. Well-indexed, they provide many genealogical clues to those who emigrated through Hamburg's port including the all-important city or German state.

There are two types of Hamburg passenger lists:

• **Direct passenger lists** are the lists of those who left Hamburg and sailed directly to their destinations without additional stops at other European ports. The lists for 1850 to 1855 are not complete, but do contain information that may be of assistance (knowing my genealogical luck, my ancestors came between 1850 and 1855 and are not on the portion of the extant lists!). The 1850 to 1855 lists are arranged alphabetically by the first letter of the surname of the

151

person identified as the head of household. After 1855, the lists are arranged chronologically based on when ships left Hamburg port.

• **Indirect passenger lists** are the lists of those who sailed from Hamburg and stopped at one or more European ports before reaching their final destination. The indirect lists are for the period 1854 to 1910; individuals who left before 1854 or after 1910 are included in the Direct passenger lists.

There are several ways of accessing the Hamburg passenger lists. In the next chapter, you'll learn how valuable the LDS Church genealogical records are. They have nearly 500 rolls of microfilm containing the passenger lists, and they are available to view by either going to the main Family History Center in Salt Lake City, or by renting them for a nominal fee and having them sent to one of their thousands of local Family History Libraries around the world. (Note, however, that Hamburg State Archives of Germany do not allow the rolls to be sent to a Family History Library in Germany. In Germany, the records must be viewed at a Hamburg State Archives location.)

Another way of reviewing information found on the Hamburg passenger lists is to visit any of several websites that offer information for a price. One I have used is *Link to Your Roots*, which is located at www.linktoyourroots.hamburg.de. As of this writing, they can do on-line searches for the years 1890 to 1908. You will be able to search their database of these years for basic information. Once you have found the name and basic information about an individual, if you want more information you have the option of paying an extra fee to get it. I searched their 1890 to 1908 database for information on my wife's ancestors, and came up with the following information from the 1896 passenger lists:

Passenger Number	Surname	First Name	State of Origin	Marital Status	Date of Birth	Destination
495083	Blau	Hannie	USA		1873/1874	New York
490134	Blau	Liebe	Osterreich		1858/1859	New York
490136	Blau	Liesel	Osterreich	Ledig	1891/1892	New York
490135	Blau	Moses	Osterreich	Ledig	1884/1885	New York
495081	Blau	Philipp	USA		1869/1870	New York
499949	Blau	Sali	Ungarn	Ledig	1879/1880	New York

Also listed were whether or not family members were in attendance with this passenger, and whether they were a Direct or Indirect passenger.

On the results of the Internet search, notice that passengers 490134, 490135 and 490136 are all named Blau. Liebe is about 38 years old, and the other two are ages 5 and 12. I think I would reasonably anticipate that this was a mother and her two children traveling together. (Can't you just see them in your mind's eye: Mother talking to the ship steward as he writes down her name and age, holding the hand of her squirming 5-year-old daughter Liesel who wants to see and experience everything going on around her, with her 12-year-old brother Moses also keeping a watchful eye on Liesel, while also trying to take in all the new sights, sounds, smells, feelings and excitement!)

Indexes
There are several indexes available to speed your research of the Direct and Indirect passenger lists.

Original. As mentioned earlier, the Direct and Indirect passenger lists for the 1850 to 1855 lists do not need indexes, as the information is already captured alphabetically by the surname of the head of household. Separate indexes for the two types of passenger lists (Direct and Indirect) exist for the periods of 1855 to 1910. One index serves the purpose for both the Direct and Indirect lists for the period between 1911 to 1914 and from 1920 to 1934. The indexes covering the period between 1855 and 1914 are arranged alphabetically by surname of the head of household, and then chronologically by the date their ship left Hamburg. Between 1920 and 1934, all the indexes are in alphabetical order.

Additional Indexes. Through the years, several additional indexes have been developed:

• **The 15-Year Index** was put together by volunteer genealogists from the LDS Church in 1969, and covers the period between 1856 and 1871. While helpful, it is important to note that they are not complete. You will also want to search in the Klüber Kartei (see below).

• **Klüber Kartei** (Klüber Card) **Index**. Hamburg genealogist Karl Werner Klüber developed a card index for the Direct passenger list for 1850 to 1871, and for the Indirect list from 1854 to 1867. The LDS Church has microfilm copies of the index. The index physically resides in the Hamburg State Archives at: Staatsarchiv Hamburg, ABS-Straße 19, D-20354 Hamburg, Germany. They will search the index for you for a fee.

The Klüber Kartei Index contains two files:

Kartei 1 (Card File 1) includes entries for Direct passenger lists from 1856 to 1871, and Indirect passenger lists from 1866 to 1867.

SECRETS OF TRACING YOUR ANCESTORS

Kartei 2 (Card File 2) includes entries for Direct passenger lists from 1850 to 1871, and Indirect passenger lists from 1854 to 1865.

You'll note that the dates for the different Klüber Kartei indexes overlap. Neither file is complete, so it is necessary to check both lists.

• **1872 Index.** Sonja Höke-Nishimoto and Daniel M. Schlyter compiled an alphabetical index of the 1872 Direct and Indirect passenger lists. It is available in microfilm from the Family History Center of the LDS Church (film 1183696, items 3-6).

To be able to use this information effectively, first decide which index is most likely to contain the information on your ancestors. Let's look first at the 15-Year Index. As mentioned above, this index covers the period between 1856 and 1871. From the matrix below, you'll select the film number that corresponds with where your ancestor's name will appear:

Name	Film Number
Aab, George to Breyer, Adam	0884668
Breytspaak, Eliza to Frick, Ludwig	0884669
Fick, Maria to Hartzke, August	0884670
Harung, Frid. to Katz, Salomon	0884671
Katz, Samual to Lewin, And.	0884672
Lewin, August to Neuer, Genofeva	0884673
Neufeld, Hoseph to Ristow, Friedr.	0884674
Ristow, H. to Schwassengewer, H.	0884675
Schwartz, Abrah. to Volkmann, A.F.W.	0884676
Volkmann, Aug. to Zyindler, Mathilde	0884677

Once you have obtained the film (either at the Family History Library in Salt Lake City or after you have ordered it and gone to one of the LDS Church's local Family History Centers), scroll down until you find the index card for your ancestor. Here's what it will look like:

SCHAUFELIN, WALTER	Metzger
Name	Occupation – Beruf

39	Hemmingen
Age — Alter	Place of Origin – Herkunftsort

Anna (Frau) 37,   Jacob 19,   Peter 17,

ETHNIC RESEARCH

Honolore 12,   Helmut 9 jahre alt

Family Members — Familienmitglieder

Other information – Sonstige Angaben

Direct / or Indirect   1858   97   12
                  Year – Jahre   Page – Seite   Code

You may have noted that the 15-Year Index and the Klüber Kartei cover essentially the same time period. However, each list is not entirely complete, so it is a good idea to check both lists. As with the 15-Year Index, when using the Klüber Kartei, select the film number for the time period that corresponds with where your ancestor's name will be. Here is the listing of the names and their film numbers:

Kartei 1
Direct - 1856 to 1871, Indirect - 1866 to 1867

Name	Film Number
Aab to Azeroth	1961710
Ba to Bethke	1961978
Bethmann to Brezzel	1961818
Bribach to Czyner	1961979
Daab to Eidenmüller	1961980
Eiding to Frei	1961981
Freiboese to Gorzewsky	1961982
Gos to Hamatuzsch	1982354
Hannauer to Herzog	1963651
Hesbenau to Jacobus	1963652
Jacoby to Kellermeyer	1963653
Kelling to Koßwitz	1917107
Kost to Lapsap	1917108
Larcher toLütscher	1917109
Lütt to Meyenburg	1964322
Meyer to Nazel	1964323
Neander to Pehmoeller	1964324
Penr to Raßner	1964325
Rast to Roszler	2012975
Rotbarth to Schmidmeier	2012976
Schmidt to Schulz E.	2013230
Schulz F. to Srock	2013305

155

Staab to Theysen	2013306
Thias to Walthusen	2013307
Walti to de Witt	2013308
Wittach to Zwocki & unknowns	201345 item 1 - 3

Kartei 2
Direct - 1850 to 1871, Indirect - 1854 to 1865

Name	Film Number
Aaener to Albersdorter	2013451 Item 4
Albert to Bemberg	2013452
Ben August to Braxmaier	2013453
Brech to Dayton	2013544
Erasmus to Gapek	2013594
Gar to Güffler	2013595
Gugel to Helwitz	2013696
Hem to Huth	2013697
Huther to Keszewsky	2013803
Ketel to Krayer	2013859
Krebeheure to Leopoldt	2013860
Lepar to Martens, H.	2014049
Martens, J. to Mohnsohn	2014050
Mohr to Oetzmann	2014051
Oetzmann to Oeverbeck	2014215
Proh to Roschke	2014216
Rose to Schlüßler	2014323
Schlüter to Schultz	2014324
Schulze to Stawizki	2014476
Stealing to Sch/Sz to Traznik	2014477
Treacks to Wezinsky	2014478
Wemmert to Zzakowitz	2014567

In addition to the 15-year and Klüber Kartei indexes, there are additional regular indexes available. These are contained in rather long lists, so they are not listed here. However, they are accessible from the LDS Family History Center or through their local Family History Libraries. You may also access the lists on-line at **home.att.net/~wee-monster/ onlinelists.html**.

Regardless of the index you use, once you find the find the ancestor you are seeking (congratulations!), use the information on the index card to find them on the indicated page of the actual passenger list. Just order the appropriate film number for the passenger list you want.

A FEW GERMAN WORDS TO EASE YOUR RESEARCH

As you go about searching the passenger lists and doing other searches through German records, the following chart will be helpful in your quest:

aunt	tante
baptism/baptized	taufe/getauft
birth	geburt
buried	vergraben
Catholic	Katholik
census	zensus
child/children	kind/kinder
church	kirche
confirmation	bestätigung
confirmed	bestätigen
county	kreis
daughter	tochter
divorced	gescheiden
father	vater
granddaughter	enkelin
grandson	enkel
grandfather	großvater
grandmother	großmutter
husband	ehemann
Lutheran	Lutherische
marriage	ehe
married	verheiratet (often abbreviated as *verh.*)
month	monat
mother	mutter
parents	eltern
parish	gemeinde
single	ledig (often abbreviated as *led.*)
son	sohn
uncle	onkel
widow	witwe
widower	witwer
widowed	verwitwet (often abbreviated as *verw.*)
wife	frau/ehefrau
year	jahre

seite _____

Verzeichniss

der Personen, welche zur Auswanderung nach _____

durch Unterzeichneten engagirt sind, und mit dem Dampf/ Segel Schiffe _____ Capitain _____

unter _____ Flagge nach _____ bedfördert weden,

Abgang des Schiffes den _____

Zurname / Die zu einer Familie gehörenden Personen sind unter einander zu notiren und durch eine Klammer als zusammengehörig zu bezeichen	Vornamen	Geschlecht männlich	Geschlecht weiblich	Alter	Bisheriger Wohnort	Im Staate resp. in der Provinz	Bisheriger Stand oder Beruf	Ziel Der Auswanderung (Ort und Land ist anzugeben)	Zahl der personen	Davon sind: Erwachsene und kinder über 10 jahre	Kinder unter 10 Jahr	Kinder unter 1 jahr
1	2	3		4	5	6	7	8	9	10	11	12

158

page ___

Index

the persons, which are immigrating to ___

whose names are written below are with the steam / sailing ship ___ Captain ___

under ___ Flag were transported to ___.

Departed on the ship on ___, 18___

The persons belonging to a family are under one another and are designated as belonging to one another		Sex		Age	Previous residence	State or the Province	Occupation	Destination of emigration (Indicate country and place)	Number of persons	Categorized as:	Children	
Surname	First name	Male	Female							Adults and children under 10 years	under 10 years	under 1 year
1	2	3		4	5	6	7	8	9	10	11	12

Once you receive the specific passenger list you have ordered, you will no doubt be excited. You race to your local Family History Library and pull up the page of the actual passenger list (see page 158). Now, unless you are a native German speaker, you may have some difficulties understanding some of the entries on the passenger list. Turn to page 159 to see an English translation of the column labels. And, to help you as you go about searching the passenger lists and doing other searches through German records, I've prepared a German-English glossary that will be useful in your quest:

Immigration Center Applications
Another gold mine of genealogical information is most commonly referred to as **EWZ files**. The *Einwanderungszentralstelle Anträge* (Immigration Center Applications) are a collection of over 400,000 applications by Germans who were living outside of Germany between 1939 and 1945. These detailed records include names of the applicant, family members and the names of their parents and grandparents. They also provide dates and places of birth for each of those individuals - just what you are searching for; it's like a genealogist designed the form! Many of the applications have extensive documentation to support their German roots - letters detailing multiple generations of German ancestors, family trees, marriage and birth certificates, etc.

These individuals claimed to be native Germans living outside of Germany and were applying to become naturalized German citizens. If one of your relatives is among the 400,000+ listed in these records, you will be fortunate indeed! If any of your relatives are not among those in the files, you may want to consider being adopted into one of these lines so you can have all this genealogical information at your fingertips! (Well, maybe not....)

Information in the EWZ files are grouped first by country or region, and then alphabetically by surname thereafter. There are nine series of files:

1. Series EWZ-50 for **Russia** (110,000 files for Germans living in the former Soviet Union; 843 rolls).
2. Series EWZ-51 for **Romania** (82,000 files on 700 rolls).
3. Series EWZ-52 for **Poland** (100,000 files for Germans living in areas within the 1939 boundaries of Poland, on 701 rolls).
4. Series EWZ-53 for the **Baltic countries** (73,000 files for Germans living in Estonia, Latvia, and Lithuania, on 587 rolls).
5. Series EWZ-541 for **Yugoslavia** (23,000 files for Germans living in regions within the 1941 boundaries of Yugoslavia, on 150 rolls).

6. Series EWZ-542 for **France** (14,000 files for Germans living in France, on 223 rolls).
7. Series EWZ-543 for **Bulgaria** (700 files for Germans living in Bulgaria, reproduced on 6 rolls)
8. Series EWZ-544 for applicants from **Wehrmacht, Organisation Todt, SD** or **SS personnel** (7,677 files for Germans living various lands, on 76 rolls).
9. Series EWZ-545 for **Süd-Tirol** (77,000 files for Germans living the area of Süd-Tirol, processed by ADERST, a forerunner of the EWZ, reproduced on 438 rolls).

Many of the EWZ files are available through the LDS Church archives. The LDS church has microfilmed most of the EWZ records, and they are available to you through visits to their Family History Center or any of the many local Family History Libraries. The **National Archives** also have a collection of the EWZ files, and they are available to purchase at $35 per roll at the time of this writing. You may contact **James Kelling**, james.kelling@arch2.nara.gov, to find out which roll holds the surname you are seeking. In the event that Mr. Kelling is promoted, transferred or retires, you may always send your inquiries to inquire@nara.gov. Once you know which ones you want, films may be ordered by calling 800/234-8861 or 202/501-5235. They accept payment by Visa or Mastercard.

Once you have located an ancestor in the EWZ files, you will also want to search the Stammblätter - family group sheets or pedigree charts. More information will likely be found there. To use the Stammblätter, look up the name of the person in the card index (E/G Kartei) to obtain the case number, then locate the case number in the record for the "Stammblätter" to obtain the film number.

If your German is a little rusty (all the records are in German), you may want to hire a professional genealogist to do some of the research for you. One who has earned a degree of respect in this area is **Ms. Rita Scheirer**, 2328 19th St., NW, Washington, DC 20009, or e-mail her at ritabill@erols.com. Fluent in German, she is intimately familiar with the EWZ files, and very well informed about the history of these records and the people they concern. Another well-regarded researcher is **Tom Stangl**. You can contact him at tstanglsr@aol.co,.

You can get more information on EWZ files by going to your Internet browser and simply typing, EWZ files. A recent search with those words yielded 801 hits. A website with good information about EWZ files is **www.genealogienetz.de/reg/DEU/ewz.html**.

Clan Books

Another wonderful source of information for German research are *Ortsippenbucher* – Clan books. Clan books are sort of like family histories of entire German towns or villages. If you are able to identify the town or area your ancestor came from, discovery of an *Ortsippenbuch* for that area may yield several generations of genealogical (and other) information about them. The information in the books is gleaned from church records, civil registries, etc., and includes birth, death, marriage and other records.

A good website about Ortsippenbuch is found at feefhs.org/igs/igs-orts.html, a website maintained by the **Federation of East European Family History Societies**. It lists all the towns and cities, by state, which have *Ortsippenbuchs* available. As you are warned at the beginning of the website, the list is a list of cities, towns, villages and counties - not surnames. To get the most information from these books, you must know the place where your ancestor came from. Virtually all the *Ortsippenbucher* are in German.

If you are stymied by the German you find in any of these documents, there are a number of fine **online German-to-English dictionaries** available. Two websites I have used extensively are www.freetranslations.com and dict.tu-chemnitz.de (note: no www. is required on the second website). The first website provides good translation of words, sentences, phrases and paragraphs. The second provides good translation services for a word or two at time. Both provide their services for free. I use the first website mostly, but whenever it gets stumped, I turn to the second website. The second website will also generally provide a number of options, including idiomatic use of the word in question.

These few websites just scratch the surface of the information available for German genealogical work. **Cyndi'sList** (www.cyndislist.com) alone lists over 216 German-specific websites for doing genealogy.

JEWISH RESEARCH

A wealth of information is available (if you know where to find it!) for those searching for their Jewish ancestors. As with all genealogical research and as has been stated before – start with what you know. Record all that you know, then poll parents, grandparents and other living relatives. Glean all the names, dates, places, copies of birth, marriage and death certificates that you can. Look especially for old letters, obituaries and journals.

ETHNIC RESEARCH

Moving beyond individuals that you know, the common sources of genealogical research come into the picture: censuses, vital statistics records kept by government offices and churches, etc. I would suggest that you go from general population records (like censuses that enumerated all individuals in the population) to records created specifically for (and often by) those of Jewish ancestry. Begin your research using the genealogy strategies and methods for the area where your family is from. There are a number of genealogical resources specific to Jewish ancestry. Some of these sources are:

- **Holocaust Records** - many records were kept on those who were imprisoned and murdered during the Holocaust. These records often assist researchers in their quest.
- **Mohel books** - books kept by mohels (circumcisers) of the work they performed. Remember, Jewish law requires that male children be circumcised when they are eight days old - which should allow you to calculate birth dates of the circumcised fairly easily. Needless to say, this will be helpful for your male ancestors only.
- **Shtetl Finders** - Shtetls are Jewish towns or communities, mostly found in eastern Europe. Shtetl Finders help identify these communities, many of which have ceased to exist.
- **Yizkor Books** - these are memorial books published by Holocaust survivors from specific towns or regions. Many of the books were written in Yiddish or Hebrew. However many translations are available. They often include the history of the communities, the memories of the communities' survivors and information about families that had no one survive the Holocaust. Generally, a listing of victims is included, along with the names and addresses of those who survived.

Perhaps because of the strong family ties of Jewish people, there are many resources available to Jewish genealogists that focus on Jews. Through the years, there seems to have been immense interest in recording information about Jewish life, traditions and families. That's the good news. The bad news is that there seem to be so many options available to researchers that it is difficult to decide which to begin with. Make no mistake: searching for your Jewish roots will provide many opportunities for you to use the sleuth-like capabilities you have (or will) develop as a genealogist.

If I were researching Jewish ancestors, after I had gotten all I could from living family members, I believe I would start with **www.jewishgen.com**. It is a wonderful, well-thought-out website dedicated to Jewish genealogy. It gives you practical advice, counsel and direction. It defines terms for you, answers frequently asked questions, and is the portal to other links and databases that will assist you immensely in your search. Here are some of the highlights of this website:

- **Jewishgen Discussion Group** - this is an e-mail-facilitated discussion group that encourages Jewish researchers to share the information they have, methods that have been successful for them in their research, case studies and ideas.
- **Jewishgen Special Interest Group mailing lists** - similar to the Discussion Group, this area focuses on specific areas (geographical or topical) and allows researchers to share the information they have, or to ask questions of those who have researched these specific areas. While not a complete list, at the time of this writing it included places like Belarus, Bohemia-Moravia, Denmark, Germany, Hungary, Latin America, Latvia and Romania. It also included topics such as Rabbinic ancestry, Yizor books, Shtetl (Jewish communities), genetic genealogy, etc.
- **The Jewishgen Family Finder** - a database of over 300,000 Jewish surnames. It is a database of ancestral towns and surnames currently being researched by Jewish genealogists worldwide. Researchers can search records submitted by others as well as submit your own surnames and towns.
- **ShtetLinks** - an infobase of over 200 stetls - Jewish communities.
- **Yizkor Book Project** - this area of the website is dedicated to unlocking the treasures that are contained in Yizkor Books. Memorials to the fallen Jews of the Holocaust, the Project is aimed at providing translation services (many Yizkor Books were originally written in Yiddish or Hebrew) and indexing work to more quickly identify individuals whose names are contained in the books.
- **Family Tree of the Jewish People** - this is a compilation of the family trees of Jewish researchers. At last count, it included the names and familial connections of over two million people.

As you can see, JewishGen is a website of immense capability and possibilities for those searching their Jewish roots.

Another outstanding website that serves as a superb resource for Jewish genealogical research is www.feefhs.org (PO Box 510898, Salt Lake City, Utah 84151-0898). The **Federation of East European Family History Societies** (FEEFHS) is an extremely active genealogical organization focused on researching the lives and histories of the people of eastern Europe, which of course includes many of Jewish ancestry. It is a conglomerate of heritage societies, archives, libraries, family groups and others who are researching their eastern European roots.

Another website with extensive information about Jewish research is that of the **LDS Church**. The LDS Church has an extensive Jewish collection, all of which is available to researchers through the Family History Library in Salt Lake City, or the local Family History Centers, branches of the Family History Library. To learn what sources are available, go to www.familysearch.org. From the home page, click on the Search the Family History Library Catalog link (it is found on the middle right-hand side of the page). From that link, select Subject Search, and type in Jewish. You'll be immediately rewarded for your efforts with a list of links to genealogical information specific to Jews. At the time of this writing, there were over 120 databases and links that contained information on Jewish research, including the Holocaust, cemeteries, biographies, newspapers and orphanages.

In recent months, FamilySeach.org has added a new item to their vast array of genealogical tools, directed especially to those who are searching their Jewish Ancestry. They have developed a research tool called Researching Your Jewish Ancestors from the United States to Europe 1850 to 1930. It is full of helpful hints and tips on how to begin and further your search for your Jewish ancestors. This 30-page research guide is available from the FamilySearch website in pdf format, and can be printed or viewed online. As mentioned throughout this book, the LDS Church's research facilities and records are available to all people interested in genealogy, regardless of religion.

AOL has a Genealogy Forum website (www.genealogyforum.com) that is helpful to those researching their Jewish roots. From the home page, click on any of several topics, and you'll be taken to a link that may be of use to you. Click on the Messages icon and you'll be taken to a message board where individuals are posting information about various individuals. Perhaps you'll find one of your ancestors hiding there. Under the same icon, look for Ethnic Resources, and click on Jewish Resources, and you'll be whisked to a host of new websites specializing in Jewish research.

Special Issues in Jewish Research
It seems like almost all ethnic groups have their own special research issues to deal with, and those searching Jewish ancestors are no different. Here are a few of the more prominent ones to be aware of:

- **Surnames**. In many parts of the world, Jews did not used fixed surnames until such usage was mandated by the government where they lived. In many instances, this was not until the late 1700s or even as late as the mid-1800s. This will of course add a certain element of difficulty to Jewish research. Prior to this, patronymics were used (the father's name was used as well as the child's given name), as well as names derived from occupations, places or even affiliation with animals. Hence the derivation of surnames like Abramson (Abram's son), Schneider (German for Tailor) or Haas (German for rabbit). These patronymics eventually evolved into surnames.
- **The Holocaust** was a tragic chapter in the history of the world and had an indelible impact on Jews and Jewish research. Entire families were wiped out, communities razed and records destroyed. There are many records that have been spawned by the Holocaust, including concentration camp records, death lists from extermination camps, Yizkor Books and others. These records help bridge the gap created by the events of the Holocaust.
- **Governments often restricted the names Jews could use**. Hebrew or Old Testament names were often specifically excluded, so Jews in those parts of the world often chose Yiddish or German names that had a symbolic association with an outlawed name.

Jewish Archival Research
Throughout the world, libraries and genealogical societies have collected (and are collecting) and are striving to preserve valuable genealogical information in the form of books, family histories, Yizkor Books, etc. There are a number of very active and very strong such organizations that focus primarily on Jewish archiving. Some of those organizations follow.

YIVO Institute for Jewish Research
Center for Jewish History
15 West 16th Street
New York, NY 10011

The YIVO Institute is one of the most respected archival organizations in the world. Their collection of records pertinent to Jewish research is impressive and second to none.

Yad Vashem Martyrs and Heroes
Remembrance Authority
PO Box 3477

91034 Jerusalem
Israel

Yad Vashem is dedicated to collecting and preserving information about the victims and survivors of the Holocaust. Their collection includes over 85,000 related to the Holocaust, including the world's largest library of yizkor books. Included at Yad Vashem are records that identify more than three million Jews who perished in the Holocaust.

Family History Library
35 North West Temple
Salt Lake City, Utah 84150
(Tel. 801/240-2331)

As detailed earlier in this section, the Family History Library of the LDS Church has a significant Jewish collection. The LDS Church has also developed a concise primer for Jewish genealogical research called Research Outline: Jewish Genealogy. This 38-page document will help you get started on researching your Jewish ancestors. It is available through the Church Distribution Center in Salt Lake City, Utah (Tel. 800/537-5950). The cost is minimal but the information is extensive.

HISPANIC RESEARCH
Although Hispanic research does not seem to be as well developed as that for other groups, it has been assisted in recent years by the development of several excellent websites. The first of these is home.att.net/~Alsosa (note that you do not use a www. prefix for this website). The brainchild of Al Sosa, the website is home for the **Hispanic Genealogy Forum**, a consortium of individuals who are actively seeking their Hispanic roots and are willing to share the fruits of their labors. Al is a gentleman who had a driving passion to learn more about his Hispanic roots. But more than that, he had a passion to share his passion. Primarily through his efforts, this website has come about.

The website is a great starting point, because it offers advice, counsel and direction in a variety of areas, and is especially helpful in putting beginning genealogists' feet on the right path. It starts off very basic, by giving you a tutorial on the terms Latin vs. Hispanic, getting started in Hispanic research, a nice section on the origin of many Hispanic names, etc. It also provides a recommendation of books and other websites that will be of assistance.

Other helpful websites include:

- www.hispanicgenealogy.com - the website of the **Hispanic Genealogy Center**, an Hispanic genealogical society of New York. It includes a number of features, including multiple message boards where you can post requests for information about a relative you simply cannot find.
- www.hispanicgen.org is the website for the **National Society of Hispanic Genealogy**. This genealogy society focuses on the ancestry and culture of Spanish-speaking peoples in the southwestern United States in the areas formerly known as New Spain and Mexico (primary links cover Colorado and New Mexico). Links to a large variety of Hispanic genealogy sites, message boards and special topics are listed on the website. You can also contact the society at National Society of Hispanic Genealogy, 924 West Colfax Avenue, Suite 104L, Denver, Colorado 80204. I really like this website.
- www.gsha.net is the website for the **Genealogical Society of Hispanic America**. This very active society is dedicated to assisting those of Hispanic ancestry research their roots. A small membership fee allows members to access scores of resources to assist their research. The society offers access to publications produced by El Escritorio (The Writing Desk), which is a publishing and research company focusing on the Hispanic, Mexican American, Chicano and Native American Communities in Colorado, New Mexico and the Borderlands.
- Another excellent Internet resource is the **AOL Hispanic Special Interest Group**, which is accessed at users.aol.com/mrosado007/index.htm (note: no www is necessary). Located in AOL's Genealogy Forum (keyword: roots), the site promotes and discusses all aspects of Hispanic genealogy. Its charter says they're not a formal society or club, and as such there is no membership fee. They serve as a very focused entry to other genealogical websites and resources. This is not the same as AOL's Genealogy Forum, www.genealogyforum.com,which is also helpful to those researching their Hispanic roots. From the home page, click on any of several topics, and you'll be taken to a link that may be of use to you. Click on the Messages icon and you'll be taken to a message board where individuals are posting information about various individuals. Perhaps you'll find one of your ancestors hiding there. Under the same icon, look for Ethnic Resources, and click on Hispanic Resources, and you'll be whisked to a host of new websites specializing in Hispanic research.
- And don't forget **Cyndi's List** (www.cyndislist.com/hispanic.htm), which serves as a nice portal to many Hispanic genealogical sites.

A FEW SPANISH WORDS TO EASE YOUR RESEARCH

If you go very far in searching for your Hispanic roots, you will run into Spanish sooner or later. Here are a few words common to genealogical research you'll want to understand:

archive	archivo
aunt	tía
baptism	bautizo, bautismo
birth	nacimiento, nacido
burial	entierro, sepultura
Catholic	Católica
census	censo
child	niño
christen	bautizo
church	iglesia
confirmation	confirmación
daughter	hija
father	padre
grandfather	abuelo
grandmother	abuela
husband	esposo
marriage	matrimonio
married	casado
month	mes
mother	madre
parents	padres
parish	parroquia
son	hijo
uncle	tío
wife	esposa, mujer
year	año

An excellent book on Hispanic genealogy is Finding Your Hispanic Roots by George R. Ryskamp (Genealogical Publishing Company, Baltimore, Maryland).

IRISH RESEARCH

Inasmuch as this is a genealogy book written by an American of Irish descent, I had to put in a section on Irish genealogical research! Here are some fairly interesting genealogical facts about Irish genealogy:

SECRETS OF TRACING YOUR ANCESTORS

• In the 2000 US Census of the United States, over 30 million Americans considered themselves of Irish descent;
• Another 40 million indicated that at least one of their progenitors was Irish;
• 70% of the travelers to Ireland each year say they have at least one Irish ancestor.

Doing Irish genealogical research can be enlightening and exhilarating. It can also be extremely frustrating. Once you leave the United States, headed back to the "ould country," you need to understand what records are available, and how to access those records.

But first - and by now you should know what I am going to say - learn all you can from your parents, grandparents, aunts, uncles, etc. From this perspective, Irish research is no different from any other ethnic research. Collect information, stories, certificates, etc. Perhaps your family has a tradition that great uncle Paddy worked on the Titanic as a welder, or that your second great grandfather lost all his family in the potato famine. Stories like these can provide clues that will help you locate your family.

Knowing a little history about Irish migration might help you pinpoint when and where your Irish ancestors came from. Many individuals assume that their Irish ancestors all came to North America during the Great Potato Famine that struck Ireland between 1845 and 1847. And they may be right. During that black chapter of Irish history, of Ireland's eight million residents in 1845, one million died and another million emigrated – most to America, although many headed for other ports of call, including Scotland, Britain, France and Australia.

But while that was a significant migration, the Irish have been seeding the world's population for many hundreds of years. My own ancestor, Teague McQuillan, left Ireland for the wilds of America in 1619, coming to Jamestown a scant 12 years after that colony was founded.

Regardless of when your Irish ancestors left the Emerald Isle, your research gets more difficult once your family roots go back to her green shores for a number of reasons. First of all, you'll discover that generations of genealogical records were destroyed during the Civil War that erupted in Ireland in 1922, a sad and lamentable fact. It ranks right up there with the burning of the 1890 US census as one of the saddest genealogical events for genealogists.

Another reason for the scarcity of records was the fact that many simply weren't kept. Vital statistics that are a genealogist's best friend (birth, marriage, death records) weren't required by the Irish government until 1864. The Catholic Church, that great genealogical organization that kept records in all its parishes throughout the world for centuries, was forbidden by Ireland's conquerors (the British) from keeping records during most of the 18th century (although many did anyway!).

But don't despair...there is hope. The Church of Ireland kept records. Land deeds were kept of land transactions, wills were kept, and several censuses were taken. Passenger lists containing the names of thousands of Irish immigrants were kept. The Irish were very clannish, and often a clan lived in the same part of Ireland for many, many generations. There are several books that will be of immense assistance in finding where your ancestors called home.

The first is *Irish Family Names* (W. W. Norton & Company, Inc., New York, NY 1989) by Brian de Breffny. Another is *The Surnames of Ireland* (Irish Academic Press Limited, 1991, Blackrock, Co. Dublin) by Edward MacLysaght. Both provide excellent listings of many Irish family names and their counties of origin. Another outstanding book on Irish families and their ancestral counties is *The Complete Book of Irish Family Names* (Irish Genealogical Foundation, 1989) by Michael C. O'Laughlin. Note: The first two books listed here are out of print, but some used ones are still offered through amazon.com.

Okay, let's say you have this craving to go to Ireland, the land of your forefathers. You want to do some real roll-up-your-sleeves research yourself. Can you do it? Of course. But first, do all you can to narrow your search before you go to Ireland. And how do you narrow your search?

First of all, you need as much of the following information as you can get:

• Surname(s) of the individual(s) you are researching
• Names of parents, siblings, spouses (including maiden names of women), etc.
• County where they came from
• City or town they lived in
• Name of the parish they lived in
• Approximate years of critical events: birth, death, marriage, etc.

Even though you are armed with that information, don't go jump on an Aer Lingus flight and head for Ireland. Know what your options are before you go. Some options are:

- **National Library of Ireland**, Kildare Street, Dublin 2, Ireland. This is the national depository of many of Ireland's records on microfilm. It specializes in Catholic parish registers. The office is open to the public, and you can go here and pore over microfilmed records to your heart's content. Before you go, write to them to determine what records they have available for the parish or diocese where your family lived - include all the information you are looking for. Most of the parish records from around the country are contained here on microfilm.
- If you know the parish where your family lived, it is possible that their names are recorded in **local parish records**. Try and locate an address and send a letter to the local clergyman, specifying the information you are seeking, and asking whether they have records that the public can peruse. Most do, some do not. Don't just show up at the priest's door with a grin on your face and a story of your search for your great aunt Bridget Murphy (note: there are many Bridgets and many Murphys in Ireland).
- **Ireland's National Archives** houses many microfilmed records from throughout Ireland, including Church of Ireland parish registries, gravestone inscriptions, census returns, probate records, deeds and a host of other records. The address is National Archives, Bishop Street, Dublin 8, Ireland.
- **The Public Record Office of Northern Ireland** has microfilms of church records of all denominations for all of Northern Ireland as well as several of the counties of the Republic. They also have many of the same secular records as the National Archives, including gravestone inscriptions, census records, old age pension claims, Tithe Applotment books, etc. Their address is Public Office of Northern Ireland, 66 Balmoral Avenue, Belfast BT9 6NY, Northern Ireland.

An alternative to doing your own research is contacting the **Irish Family History Foundation**. It is a network of genealogical research centers in the Republic of Ireland and in Northern Ireland which have computerized millions of Irish ancestral records. For a fee, they will do a search for your family in the records for their part of the country. Their main website is www.irishroots.net (catchy, don't you think?). There are Research Centers for each of the counties for Ireland and Northern Ireland, and they will search the most common records for information about your family. As of this writing, for a fee of about $70, an initial search will be made of available records for the area to determine if your family was from that area. If they were, and you wish it, for $230 (and up), the Research Center will do a comprehensive history of your family in that part of the country.

Before you go rushing off to Ireland to do your genealogy (it is a good excuse to go to Ireland though!), first check with your local Family History Center of the **LDS Church** to see what Irish records they may have. As of this writing, here is what was available to assist in your Irish research (unless otherwise noted, records are for both Ireland and Northern Ireland):

• Microfilmed indexes of births, marriages and deaths through 1958;
• Pre-1871 marriage and death certificates;
• Birth certificates from 1864 to March 1881 and from 1900 to 1913;
• Birth certificates for Ireland from 1930 through 1955;
• Birth, marriage and death certificates for Northern Ireland from 1922 through 1959.
• Deeds and tax records
• Census records
• Estate and probate records
• Family histories
• Occupational and school records
• Military service records

Along with other miscellaneous records and family histories, the **Family History Library** in Salt Lake City has more than 3,000 books, over 11,500 microfilms and 3,000 microfiche containing information about the people of Ireland. Virtually all of these records are available to you no matter where you live by making a visit to the Family History Center at the local LDS chapel nearest where to you live.

A publication entitled *Research Outline: Ireland* is available from the LDS Church Distribution Center for a nominal fee. It is an outstanding overview of research strategies, available records, and recommendations to make your Irish genealogical search a successful one. You may contact the Distribution Center by calling them at 800/537-5950.

AOL has a Genealogy Forum website (www.genealogyforum.com) that is helpful to those researching their Irish roots. From the home page, click on any of several topics, and you'll be taken to a link that may be of use to you. Click on the Messages icon and you'll be taken to a message board where individuals are posting information about various individuals. Perhaps you'll find one of your ancestors hiding there. Under the same icon, look for Ethnic Resources, and click on Irish Resources, and you'll be whisked to a host of new websites specializing in Irish research.

OTHER ETHNIC-SPECIFIC RESEARCH

As much as I would like to address specific research techniques and help uncover sources of information for the countless other ethnic groups, it is simply beyond the scope of a volume this size. However, here are a few tips that may yield results for you.

From your Internet search engine, type the name of your ethnic group or the country from which the ancestor you are searching came, followed by the word genealogy (for example: Scandinavian genealogy, German genealogy, Chile genealogy, etc.). You'll be surprised at the number of websites you find that are dedicated to these areas of genealogy. And more often than not, many of those websites will have links to other websites that will also be focused on the area of the world or the ethnicity you are seeking.

Go to your local library and visit their genealogy section. They will likely have at least a few books on the areas of research you are seeking. If they do not have a particular book, inter-library loans can almost always be arranged so that you can get the books to review.

Find your local Family History Center. They will provide a gateway to the largest genealogy library in the world. You can go to the FamilySearch website (www.familysearch.org) to search for the Family History Center nearest to you.

Check out family history organizations, genealogy societies, etc. that have been formed to further research on a particular family name or for a particular country. You may find these on the Internet, in your local library, or in the phone book.

Learn the history of the peoples or countries you are researching. A knowledge of the history of a particular ethnic group or country will help you understand things that may assist your research. For example, if the family tradition is that your great uncle Paddy came to America as a ten year old when his family all died in the Great Potato Famine in Ireland, then you immediately know that he was probably born between 1835 and 1837. If you know the dates of the Great Potato Famine (1845 to 1847) you can easily calculate that he must have been born about ten years earlier. That is a good clue with which to begin - or further - your search.

Traveling to Unearth Your Roots

Even though records are available via the Internet and on microfilm and microfiche, if you are able to travel to the land of your ancestors' nativity, it is a wonderful experience that will likely live long in your memory. But before you go, here are a few suggestions that will make your trip a little more enjoyable, and hopefully, a little more fruitful from a genealogical standpoint:

• Do all you can to pinpoint what part of the country your relatives came from. Don't just show up in the country and hope to find where they lived. Find their town or county if at all possible.
• If at all possible, contact distant relatives living in the same part of the country where your relatives came from. Because of the research he had done, Alex Haley, the author of Roots, was able to locate the obscure African village where his ancestors came from, and he was able to visit there and establish a link with his past.
• Before you go, gather as many of your genealogical documents as you can that might be of assistance to you during your journey. Documents that list dates and places are particularly useful. Don't rely on your memory alone to guide you. Parish names, towns, counties, etc. are all clues that may help you locate the place of your ancestors' births and lives. (Note: make copies of these documents - you don't want to lose them in redirected luggage!)
• Determine beforehand how you will travel in the country you are visiting. Does rail service go to the area of the country you wish to travel to? How about bus service? Or would a rental car better serve your needs?
• Before going, try to locate where original records might be kept. Are they kept in the local parish church, or have the records been centralized to a national or county office or someplace else? Are they accessible, and if so, what hours are they available?

One of the most remarkable genealogical experiences I have had was when I traveled to the land of my forefathers - Ireland. Five of my eight great grandparents' surnames are Irish, so I have a special fondness for the Emerald Isle in my heart. Before my first trip there, I decided to try and contact some long-lost cousins. Never shy, I decided on a bold plan. First of all, it required a letter written to my Irish cousins. This is what I wrote:

Dear McQuillan Family,
Greetings from your long-lost American cousin! Doubtless you were unaware that you had a long-lost American cousin, at least not this one. But you do. In 1619 my tenth-great grandfather Teague McQuillan left County Antrim to see if he could improve his fortunes in the wilds of America. Ten generations later here I am, intensely interested in visiting the part of Ireland he left so long ago. But that's not all. I am as interested in meeting other members of the McQuillan family as I am in seeing the Emerald Isle. Hence my letter. In May of next year,

my wife and I are planning to visit Ireland and would like to be able to visit some of the cousins as well as the part of Ireland Teague was from. We will be in Northern Ireland from May 3 through May 10, and would love to stop by and meet you. Please let me know if you will be available during that time, and we'll arrange our schedule to meet with you.

I know this may seem rather presumptuous and just a bit bold, but I really am interested in meeting other members of the McQuillan Clan, however distant along the family tree they may be. Thanks, and I look forward to meeting with you when we are there.

- Daniel Quillen

After I wrote the letter, I made twenty copies. Then, from a map of Northern Ireland, I selected twenty small towns in County Antrim, where my ancestor was from. (I think something like this will work better with small towns rather than larger cities.) I addressed each envelope with the family name and the name of one of the towns. For example, one of the letters was addressed as follows: McQuillan Family, Larne, Northern Ireland.

And then, in the bottom left-hand corner of the front of the envelope I wrote: POSTMASTER: PLEASE DELIVER THIS LETTER TO ANY McQUILLAN FAMILY IN THE VICINITY.

I sent the letters six months prior to our trip to Ireland. I was delighted to receive seven responses to my rather unorthodox method of contacting family. But the results were marvelous! We met a number of these Irish families, were entertained in their homes, and they showed us great kindness. We left much richer for our time with them.

As a special bonus, they provided us with a wonderful genealogical treasure. Literally hundreds of names were provided to us, members of the family that I had not previously known about. They took us to the "old homestead," prowled through graveyards with us helping us locate the gravestones of past relatives, and a dozen other genealogical kindnesses. In fact, they introduced us to the "County Genealogist." He was a man whose father had prided himself in knowing all there was to know about all the principal families of the county, and who had passed the genealogical baton on to his son before his death. The son – the latest County Genealogist – was able to share stories about the family, and even provided copies of articles that had been written through the years about the medieval adventures of several of my ancestors.

So, if you are of Irish extraction, give it a try. I can vouch for its success in Ireland. If you are not Irish (how sad - but I suppose not everyone is so fortunate), try it with the land of your ancestors' nativity. What's the worst thing that could happen? The main risk, as I see it, is that the letters might be tossed in the garbage by postal workers who don't want to be bothered. But what if they are delivered? What if a distant relative responds? Cousin or not, you're sure to meet some wonderful people, and you'll likely establish some long-lasting friendships.

Ethnic Research Checklist

___ Identify an ancestor you would like to do research for.

___ Decide what you want to learn about him or her.

___ Write down everything you know about this ancestor - names, dates, locations, etc. Include information gleaned from family traditions.

___ Understand what ethnic research records are available to research.

___ Understand the process for accessing the various ethnic research sources (Internet, periodicals, genealogical societies, books, etc.).

___ If you are traveling to the land of your ancestors' nativity, make copies of all the genealogical information you have.

Additional Resources

Blankenship, Bob, Cherokee Roots, Volume 1 & 2: Western Cherokee Rolls, Cherokee Roots, 2nd edition (June 1992)

Burroughs, Tony, Black Roots: A Beginners Guide to Tracing the African-American Family Tree, Fireside Books, (February 2001)

de Breffny, Brian, Irish Family Names, W. W. Norton & Company, Inc., New York, NY (1989)

Gormley, Myra Vanderpool Cherokee Connections, Genealogical Publishing Company (January 2002)

Howell, Barbara Thompson, How to Trace Your African-American Roots: Discovering Your Unique History, Citadel Printing (January 1999)

MacLysaght, Edward, The Surnames of Ireland, Irish Academic Press Limited (1991)

McClure, Tony Mack, Cherokee Proud, Chu-Nan-Nee Books, 2nd edition (1998)

O'Laughlin, Michael C. The Complete Book of Irish Family Names, Irish Genealogical Foundation (1989)

Ryskamp, George R. Ryskamp, Finding Your Hispanic Roots, Genealogical Publishing Company.

Woodtor, Dee Parmer, Finding a Place Called Home: A Guide to African-American Genealogy and Historical Identity, Random House Publishing (1999)

Research Outline: Jewish Genealogy, Church of Jesus Christ of Latter-day Saints

14. WHO AM I?

The Genealogical Dilemma of Adoption
So you are -- or one of your ancestors is -- adopted. The genealogical question for you is simply, "Which line should you research?" Unfortunately, the question may be a lot easier than the answer (the story of my life, it seems!). Depending on you, your motivation and desires, the answer could be any of the following:

• your adopted line
• your birth line
• both your birth and adopted lines

Your adopted line - Many of those I know who have been adopted consider that family their family and the only one it makes sense for them to do research on. And that is perfectly fine.

Your birth line - There will be many who, though perfectly satisfied with their adopted family, will choose to want to do family research on their birth line - the ancestors of the parents who gave them up for adoption. Sometimes adoptions are "open" and individuals will know from a very early age who their birth parents are. More often than not, however, those adoptions are not open, and the task is to first find who their birth parents (or birth grandparents, etc.) are.

There are many reasons why an individual who has been adopted may want to research their birth line - natural curiosity, a desire to learn about their health history, or as varied as the number of adoptees out there.

Both your birth and adopted lines - For all the reasons listed above, adoptees may wish to research both lines.

Whatever your motivation, whatever your desires, if you choose to research your birth line, you add another level of complexity to your search for ancestors. First and foremost, you need to identify those who physically brought you into this world. Often, your quest will be to find the birth parents of your grandparents, great-grandparents or beyond. This chapter will address some sources that may be helpful to you as you seek to peel off this first layer of the genealogical onion.

Where to Start?

As with most other areas of genealogical research, start with what you know. Write down every bit of information you are personally aware of as it pertains to the adoption in question. While this may seem obvious, the first place to look is your birth certificate (or the birth certificate for the ancestor for whom you are seeking birth parents). It may contain the name of your birth parents. If not, it will at least provide the date and place of your birth - both important clues in your research.

Once you exhaust all the information you personally know, expand your circle to others who may know - parents, grandparents, aunts and uncles. Remember - don't forget great-aunt Ruth, who is the member of the family that has an affinity for genealogy. Probe their memories for whatever information they may remember. Write it all down - they may be clues that are meaningless, but there might also be the key that unlocks the door to the mystery you are seeking to solve.

How old were you when you were adopted? Were you adopted as an infant, or sometime later? Were your birth parents from the same city or state where you were adopted (this is often the case)? Your adopting parents or extended relatives may be able to provide answers to these questions.

Especially if you were adopted some years after your birth, then my suggestion is to get the newspapers for the locality of your birth for the dates immediately around your birthdate. Did any of them list the babies born on the day of your birth? Or perhaps births were listed only once a week or once per month. While doing research on a great-uncle of mine, I discovered that the local county newspaper listed all births that occurred during the previous year in the first newspaper of the new year. Now, understand that the baby's name - first as well as last - may be entirely different than the name you now carry. Many families rename their infant and toddler children. But if you find a number of births on the day of your birth, then make a list of the names of the parents who are listed. None of them may pan out, but maybe....

Back to your parents -- they may be able to provide you valuable

WHO AM I?

information that will assist you in your research. Even if the adoption was a closed adoption, they may remember some details that will narrow your search. Things like:

• the city of the adoption agency;
• whether your birth mother was married;
• the hospital you were born in;
• whether your birth mother had any other children
• if so, were they also adopted?
• what was the name of the adoption agency
• was it a government agency?
• was it a church-affiliated adoption agency?
• and so on ...

Look for any information you can get - even the most seemingly inconsequential. That little piece of information might well lead you to the key that opens the adoption door for you.

Once you have gleaned all the information from the sources closest to you, it is time to look elsewhere. Your next stop should be the Agency or state that handled your adoption. If your adoption was a closed adoption, they will not be able to provide you a lot of information. However, ask for your non-identifying information.

This will provide a little information about your adoption. While it won't provide the names of your birth parents, it may provide clues about where to look for them. Non-identifying information is health and other information about your background that is generally gathered and made available to all members involved in the adoption. Information varies by agency and state, but you may be able to receive information such as medical history (known diseases, pertinent information about the adopted child's pregnancy, and any special medical issues), social history such as ethnicity, age of birth parents, whether the birth parents were married, religion and educational backgrounds. If available, some agencies provide information about the birth parents' interests.

Note: Hawaii and Kansas are the only states (thus far) that allow adult adoptees full access to their adoption records.

While none of this information will provide you names, addresses or contact information, it may provide clues to assist you in narrowing your search.

Once you have exhausted those resources closest to you, and have gleaned all you could from the adoption agency, it is time to expand your research to a broader and less personal arena: the Internet. As you know by now, the Internet is a tremendously effective tool for genealogical researchers.

CYNDI'S LIST

One of the best places to initiate your search for adoption information is that ever-popular and very helpful website, Cyndi's List: www.cyndislist.com. A quick visit to Cyndi's List yielded over 125 different websites that provided assistance in finding long-lost relatives through an adoption situation. Here are a few that impressed me:

Adoptee Birthfamily Connections: www.birthfamily.com. This website specializes in reuniting families separated by adoption. I liked their tagline - Expect Miracles.

Adoptee's Search Handbook: www.ouareau.com/adoptee/index.html. This website is authored by Madelene Ferguson Allen, an adopted child herself. She states that the intent of the website is to help individuals find their families. Focused primarily on searches in Canada, it nevertheless has some excellent source suggestions that can be of help to individuals elsewhere.

AdoptioNetwork: http://www.adoption.org. This multi-dimensional website features many aspects of adoption, including reuniting families (select Reunite from the home page). (Also called Adoption.org)

Adoption Puzzle: www.genealogytoday.com/adoption/puzzle. This wonderful website is a wealth of knowledge, covering information from adoptees' rights and legal issues to a registry for those seeking to be reunited with their family members.

BirthQuest: www.birthquest.org. This organization is devoted to searching for adoptees, birth parents, adoptive parents and siblings.

Families Lost: www.familieslost.com. This site provides a registry, resources and how-to's, message boards, etc.

Lia's Links: www.rootexinc.net/LiasLinks.html. This site lists nearly 200 sites for you to register your search.

Looking 4 Kin–Adoption Genealogy Links: www.looking4kin.com/

WHO AM I?

adpt.htm. As the name implies, this site lists a number of genealogy websites that might assist you in your search.

Orphan's Home Website: freepages.genealogy.rootsweb.com/ ~orphanshome/ welcome.htm. This outstanding website provides transcriptions of orphanages that were listed on censuses throughout the years. This is an outstanding place to search for ancestors who may have stopped briefly (or not so briefly) in an orphanage prior to being adopted - or prior to growing out of the orphanage.

Searching for Birth Relatives: www.adoptions.com/aecsearch.html. This excellent site provides common sense instruction and resources for conducting your search.

REGISTRIES

There are many, many registries on the Internet where you can register as one seeking to contact your birth family. It is interesting how often both parties of an adoption - those who gave the child up for adoption as well as the adopted child - concurrently yearn to make contact with one another. These registries provide a clearinghouse for those kinds of reunions to be accomplished. As an adoptee, you will list your contact information. Hopefully the individuals you are seeking do the same!

There are websites where you can register your name or the name of the ancestor for whom you are searching. Some of the better ones include:

Adoptee Birthfamily Connections: www.birthfamily.com/contacts.htm. This is one of the better-known sites among adoption websites.

Adoptee Contact Line: www.adoptees-contact-line.com very nice, personal website focused on reuniting adoptees and birth parents.

Adoption Registry: www.registry.adoption.com/form_a.php. This website purports to be the largest adoption registry out there, with nearly 300,000 people in their database as of this writing. (It is the largest I have found thus far.)

Birthday Search: www.skylace.net/adoption/searchbirthday.html - search for adoptions bases on birthdates of the adoptee.

Black Market Registry: www.geocities.com/Heartland/Garden/2313/ index.htm. This site focuses on reuniting families where adoption was on the Black market - illegal.

SECRETS OF TRACING YOUR ANCESTORS

Canadian Adoptees Registry: www.canadianadopteesregistry.org/ index.html. As the name implies, this site focuses on Canadian adoptees. Nearly 34,000 individuals are in their database.

International Soundex Reunion Registry: www.plumsite.com/isrr. This site purports to be one of the largest registries for adoption.

Kindred Pursuits: www.kindredpursuits.org (I love the name of this agency.) About 60% of those registered are Canadian and the other 40% are American.

Links: members.shaw.ca/rkading/ (Note the lack of www on this website.) Another site focused on Canadian adoptions.

Merry Go Round International Adoption Search Registry: www.geocities.com/Heartland/Garden/1145/post.htm.

Metro Reunion Registry: www.detective-net.com/adoption.html. This site provides a list of state- and province-specific adoption registry services. Their tag line is, We Deserve a Complete Family Tree.

Parent Finders of Canada: www.parentfinders.org. A similar organization operates in various states in the United States.

Candice Johnn's Relinquished: freeweb.wpdcorp.com/relinquished. Focusing on adoptions conducted through the Catholic church, it has an extensive database available.

When you contact these registries and provide your information, if registry finds a possible match for you, they will contact you to determine if you want to contact or be contacted. They should not provide your information to others without your express permission. Check their bylaws or instructions to ensure this is the case before you register. If you do register with one or more of these registries, it is important to keep your information updated: telephone numbers, e-mail addresses, etc. What a tragedy it would be to register with a registry where your kin is also registered, only to not be able to be contacted because your contact information was not updated!

OTHER RESOURCES
In addition to the Internet, there are items that may assist you in your quest to identify birth parents or beyond: they are called books. In my research I stumbled across the website located at www.members.aol.com/

wmlgage/ll/Searching.html. It provided a list of books that assisted the search for adopted families.

Another resource is **People Searching News**. This organization, whose mission is to reunite birth parents and adoptees, has a National Search Hotline (Tel. 407/768-2222). Calls to the hotline will be given solid information on how to begin and conduct your search. They will also send you a free list of books and articles that will assist you. They partner with over 2,000 search and support groups for research and reunion registries. You may also write to them for information at People Searching News, PO Box 100-444, Palm Bay, Florida 32910. Include a self-addressed stamped envelope with your request.

If you are aware of the area of the country where your family lived, you might try placing an ad in a local newspaper. Something along the lines of:

Wanted: Information about Bobbie E. Jones. Born around 1940 in or around Grangeville. Mr. Jones is my grandfather, and was adopted through the local Catholic parish in 1942. I am seeking information about my grandfather's birth family. If you have any information at all, please contact me at _____.

Message Boards. These wonders of the Internet provide useful sites to search for family members. I entered "Adoption Message Boards" into my Internet search engine and got nearly 2,000,000 hits! Many weren't exactly what I was looking for, but many others were in fact message boards dealing with adoptions and seeking to reunite families. I'd suggest using a number of them.

AFTER YOU'VE FOUND A NAME
There are two parts of the adoption process - first locating the name of the family who gave the child up for adoption, then finding the family (or their descendants) themselves. To do this, utilize any of the research techniques that have been discussed in this book - family members, vital statistics records, obituaries, newspapers, etc., etc.

One we have not discussed is the **Social Security system**. If you have reason to believe that the person you are seeking is still alive, try this: Write a letter to this person, explaining who you are and why you have been looking for them. Be sure and include your contact information! Place the letter in an unsealed envelope with the person's name on it. Then write another letter to the Social Security Research department.

Explain who you are, your relation to the person whom you are seeking, and ask for them to forward your letter to the person. Send your letters to:

Social Security Research
401 Connecticut Avenue NW Room 205
Washington DC 20008-2304

And then wait! Also, there is a $5 charge for this service, so include a check for that amount.

Before you prepare your letter, check the Social Security Death Index. Certainly you are hoping this person won't show up there! However, if they do, then you may find additional clues as to where to continue your search for others that might be of assistance to you. The Social Security Death Index will list the individual's name, birth and death dates, last residence and where the original social security number was applied for - all great genealogical clues to helping you find more information that might lead you to what you are looking for.

Locality-Specific Adoption Help
Every state I checked had an adoption organization specific to their state. Trips to their websites provided information about resources available within the state and nationwide, the law as it applies to those searching for birth parents or adoptees. Some provided additional resources, like recommended books and articles, other helpful websites and location-specific registries.

To access these sites, just type into your browser the following: (Location) adoption; for example: Colorado Adoption.

SHOULD I PAY SOMEONE TO SEARCH FOR ME?
Well, that is a good question. Understand that there are agencies out there that will – for a fee – do the detective work to try and find your birth parents or the birth parents of an ancestor. Some of these businesses can cost great sums of money. If you have exhausted all other avenues, or simply do not have the time but do have the money, you may consider using a professional researcher to assist you in your quest.

Special note on this chapter: this chapter was not in the first edition of Secrets of Tracing Your Ancestors. It is here specifically because I was contacted by numerous individuals - readers of the first edition - who were seeking information on how to research for their adoptive families.

WHO AM I?

As I assisted them in locating information on how to search it occurred to me that this might be a helpful chapter for others.

Who Am I? Checklist
___ Determine whether you want to do research on your adoptive family or your birth parent line.

___ Write down all available information that you currently have.

___ Are there others within your current family circle that might have additional clues about your adoption, or the adoption of an ancestor?

___ Seek out additional resources that may be of help - websites, books, adoption agencies, message boards, etc.

___ Be persistent - don't get discouraged!

Additional Resources
Julie Jarrell Bailey, N Lynn Giddens and Annette Baran, The Adoption Reunion Survival Guide: Preparing Yourself for the Search, Reunion and Bryond (New Harbinger Publications, 2001)

Joseph J Culligan, Adoption Searches Made Easier (FJA Publishing, 1995)

Carol Ann Gray, How to Find Your Past: A Search Handbook for Adoptees (Pamphlet Publication)

Mary Jo Rillera, The Adoption Searchbook: Techniques for Searching People, (Pure CA, third edition, 1991)

C Curry Wolf, The Blue Book 2000, The Adoption Re-Connection Directory, Search & Support Referral Source (Wolf Publishing, 2000)

15. USING DNA AS A RESEARCH TOOL

Surely you've heard of Deoxyribonucleic Acid. If that doesn't ring a bell, then perhaps you know it by its more common nomenclature: **DNA**. If you have watched any of the police reality TV shows that have been popular in recent years, you have surely heard about DNA's use in helping pinpoint bad guys. You know the scene: the detective is trying to find out who was responsible for a heinous crime. Several suspects have been identified, but they all seem to have iron-clad alibis. Or do they? Then some hair is discovered at the crime scene that doesn't belong to the victim or any of their family members, but looks a lot like it might belong to one of the suspects. The suspect gives up a lock of his hair or a swab of saliva; a DNA test is performed, and *voila!* – a 99.8% probability that the hair came from the suspect. The jury is persuaded and the suspect goes to prison for a long time. Case closed.

So why a chapter on DNA in a book on genealogy? Can you use it to identify your ancestors. No. Well, maybe. Well, not exactly, but it can be useful. Huh? Read on.

First of all, the previous chapter dealt with searching out birth parents in an adoption situation. If the connection is close enough – parent or grandparent, then DNA could definitely be used to verify with surety the relationship between individuals.

But we are talking about using DNA in genealogical research that goes back numerous – perhaps many – generations. Let me explain.

Using DNA in genealogical research (called *genetealogy* by Megan Smolenyak, a pioneer in this area) is gaining traction among scientists and genealogists alike. Read on to see what it means:

USING DNA AS A RESEARCH TOOL

Without going into too much scientific depth (your ninth grade science class on DNA should suffice), let me explain. DNA is the chemical inside the cells that make up human beings. These cells carry the genetic instructions for forming humans: their hair and eye color, height, build, tendency towards certain diseases, etc. Chromosomes are segments of DNA that contain genes, the basic unit of heredity. Each of us received one set of 23 chromosomes from each of our parents.

One of those chromosomes – the 23rd one – determines our sex. Mothers contribute an X chromosome and fathers contribute either an X or a Y chromosome to the baby-building equation. If the father contributes an X chromosome to the X chromosome contributed by the mother, the child is a girl; if he contributes a Y chromosome then the child is a boy. (Remember poor Henry VIII, who kept blaming his wives for their inability to conceive boys? We now know it was his fault, not theirs.)

Scientists have discovered that a portion of the Y chromosome is passed from father to son to grandson and beyond, with little or no change. So that wee portion of the Y chromosome will be nearly identical in the son, father, grandfather, great-grandfather, etc., all the way, I suppose, to Father Adam (through Noah, of course, and assuming an unbroken paternal line!). Tests have been developed that can isolate this area and determine whether two male individuals are related, even though they are separated by many generations.

Another type of DNA, called mitochondrial DNA (mtDNA) is similarly passed identically from mothers to their sons and daughters. It stops with the sons, but continues with the daughters.

There is yet one other test that can be run on DNA that is useful for genealogists. It is a test of the Ancestral Markers of the DNA – called Single Nucleotide Polymorphisms (SNPs). This test identifies the geographic region of the world that the tested person's DNA comes from. These tests will yield a percentage: 33% South American, 60% Eastern European, 7% West Africa, for example.

So that all sounds fine and good, but what does that mean for you and me and our ancestral research? Let's start with the most logical and work into the more vague areas.

We mentioned earlier that DNA can be used to confirm a connection to birth parents or beyond. An example might be that you are adopted and think you may have located your birth parents. But there is a question or

189

two that just doesn't seem right – your birth parents are both dark haired and you are blonde; they gave a child up for adoption in North Dakota, but you were adopted in Alabama. Either a DNA or mtDNA test would prove the relationship. If you are a male, you will have the same Y DNA that your father had – almost if not exactly identical. But what if your father isn't known, or passed away many years ago? Then you would turn to the mtDNA test – remember, mothers pass this identical information to their sons and daughters. If there is a match – congratulations you found your mother.

Here's another scenario: Your grandfather was adopted, and you want to research both his adopted family and his birth parents. You think you have identified his birth parents, but there are no records – just family tradition which says your grandfather was raised by a family in the same town as his birth parents. And – both of your grandfather's suspected birth parents have passed away. What to do next?

Applying your ninth-grade science knowledge (with perhaps a little brush up from this chapter), you reason that if the suspected father had any brothers, and they had any male children, and they had male children, then those children would have the same Y chromosome DNA as you have (or the same DNA your mother has, if you are a woman). So you find the suspected birth father's brother (who has of course passed away long ago), and identify a grandson of his who lives in a nearby town. You contact him, explain your dilemma, and he agrees to help. You both take the Y DNA test and.....your DNA is identical – hello, cousin, mystery solved.

Another use for DNA is to determine if two individuals (fellow genealogists, no doubt) tie into a common ancestor. If you are both men, this should be a piece of cake. You both have the same surname. You are both males. If you tie into a common ancestor, you will both have the same Y DNA results. (Remember, fathers pass the same Y DNA onto their sons, who pass it on to their sons, etc.)

Similarly, if you both have similar surnames but spelled differently, here is a way to determine if you are related. For example, I communicate with a fellow genealogist whose surname is McQuillan. My research has indicated that once upon a time, my family's surname was McQuillan. If he and I are related through a common paternal ancestor, since we are both males, that small section of our Y DNA that is tested will be identical. Finally, let's say that as you have researched a line you have hit a brick wall. Let's further say that you find yourself at a crossroads – some

USING DNA AS A RESEARCH TOOL

research you have done indicates a possible northern European connection. But you also have some clues that your ancestors came from South America. Maybe testing your Ancestral Markers will give you a clue which direction you should forge ahead in. Several dozen specific geographic areas of the world have thus far been identified through Ancestral Markers.

Pretty exciting stuff, huh?

Okay, so I have interested you. What's next – where do you go to learn more? For starters, there is one exceptional website I have found that provides a lot of information, answers a lot of questions, and directs you to more websites to learn even more information. The website is **www.duerinck.com/surname.html**. This marvelous website features the DNA testing project for the Duerinck surname. Or perhaps someone is already doing research on your surname. To find out if this is possible, go to **www.dnalist.net**, which provides a database of surname projects that are underway. For a list of labs providing tests, visit **www.clanlindsay.com/new_page_4.htm**. Or you can just type "DNA Testing Labs" into your browser and *voila* – more labs than you can shake a Y chromosome at!

"How much will it cost?" you ask. Well, its not cheap, but neither is it unspeakably expensive. There are a variety of tests, but they run between $99 and $300, depending on the test you are requesting, whether just one or more people are being tested, etc.

Using DNA as a Research Tool Checklist
___ Do you have a situation where DNA testing and research might help?

___ Determine how the DNA would flow (father to son, mother to son/daughter) and determine whether you can make an unbroken connection back to the person in question.

___ Check to see if the potential distant cousin is amenable to DNA testing – philosophically as well as financially. (Note: if it is really important to you, you may offer to pay all costs.)

___ Identify a DNA testing lab that performs these sorts of DNA tests.

___ Be persistent – don't get discouraged!

Additional Resources

http://www.relativegenetics.com — the website for Relative Genetics, a testing lab that is dedicated to welding genealogical research with DNA testing.

http://www.oxfordancestors.com - this is the website for Oxford Ancestors, which is associated with Dr. Bryan Sykes, one of the pioneers of DNA testing for genealogical purposes.

http://www.familytreedna.com — the website for Family Tree DNA.

Family Chronicle magazine runs articles on using DNA and genealogical research every so often. Here are a few articles that have run there that should be of interest:

• *Genealogy and Genetics: Marital Bliss or Shotgun Wedding?* (March/April 2003, pages 20 — 23)
• Megan Smolenyak, *Managing a DNA Project*, September/October 2003, pages 17 — 20)
• S.C. Meates *Genetic Genealogy Basics*, May/June 2004, pages 27 – 28)
• Sykes, Bryan, *The Seven Daughters of Eve*, New York: W. W. Norton & Co. (2000)
• Carmichael, T. and Kuklin, A., *How to DNA Test Our Family Relationships*, (Mountain View, CA, Ace Press, (2000)

16. IS ANYONE OUT THERE?

Undoubtedly, as you begin researching your family tree, you will run across other genealogists who are also interested in some of your ancestors. It may be an aunt you didn't know had an interest in genealogy, or it may be a distant cousin who happened to tie into your family through marriage. Regardless, sometimes these chance encounters can result in moving far beyond where you are on the family tree, or allowing that person to move far beyond where they currently are in their research on the family tree. Either way, it is a win-win situation for both individuals.

Don't pass on the opportunity to strike up a conversation with these fellow genealogists. They may have access to information you don't have. No matter how good you have gotten at ferreting out information from courthouses, census records, vital statistics, etc., these individuals may have things like old family Bibles, family papers like divorce papers, military discharges, marriage licenses, etc. And when you have information like this, there is an incredible sense of satisfaction in sharing it. Networking and sharing research are two of the hallmarks of successful genealogists.

Consider the following example that happened while I was researching this book. In an effort to provide meaningful examples to share with my readers, I was trying to pin down some additional information on my great grandfather. As detailed in the chapter on censuses, I began to think that he was born in Tennessee. The most likely location was Sullivan County, Tennessee, as that is where his father was born, and it was right across the state line from where my great grandfather grew up.

While searching the Internet for clues, I came across a website for the Sullivan County, Tennessee Genealogy Society. As I checked it out, I saw that they had a list of the surnames their members were working on, and my surname was among them. It also provided the name and e-mail address of the individual who was working on the Quillen line. I fired off an e-mail to him introducing myself. He responded almost immediately, and we determined that his 3rd great grandfather was my 4th great grandfather. He also indicated that he used **Personal Ancestral File (PAF) software**, and that if I had compatible software he would be happy to send me the genealogical records he had. I responded affirmatively, and within a day he sent me a large file containing all the individuals for whom he had done research – over 33,000 names, over 3,600 of whom had the surname Quillen!

So how do you contact individuals who are working on your line of the family? Sometimes when you run across them, you'll find only a name of the researcher with no address. Sometimes the address that you discover is many years and several expired forwarding address cards old. What then? Or – what if you want to see if there is anyone out there who is working on your line?

There are a number of avenues to pursue in searching for fellow genealogists. Following are a couple that I have had success with.

The Internet
Once again, this juggernaut of genealogical research comes to the aid of genealogists. Numerous websites provide an effective and relatively accurate means of identifying and contacting fellow genealogists, as well as contacting members of the family that might be able to provide information on an ancestor. These website are excellent electronic versions of the white pages of your local directory. Except they provide you access to the white pages in any locality in the nation. Several that I have used to locate others are **www.people.yahoo.com**, **www.switchboard.com**, and **www.whitepages.com**. The first two also allow you to search for e-mail addresses.

So how do these work, and how do you use them? While writing this book I was also doing some genealogical research on one of my family lines. I found that someone had been working on one of my lines. He had placed a query on a message board looking for information about members of my family. Unfortunately, he had placed this query on the message board a year ago, and the e-mail address he posted was no longer working. I noticed that the e-mail address looked like his initials and his last name. Armed with that little bit of information, I went to one of the above-mentioned websites. With just a few keystrokes, I found both his home and e-mail addresses as well as his home phone. To get this information, I just searched in the states surrounding the area where people generally are from who do research on my family. We were able to connect with one another and share information.

Message Boards
Message boards are websites where individuals place queries, specifying information or families they are searching for. For example, the following message was on a message board I visited recently:

Surnames: Quillen, Burke
Classification: Query
Subject: Sarah Minerva Burke married to Jonathan Baldwin Quillen

My great grandmother was Sarah Minerva Burke and she married Jonathan Baldwin QUILLEN. I think her her mother was Emeline??? and her father Thomas Burke. I don't even know their location for sure except they married in Lee Co. Virginia, and had children in TENN, and KY, possibly AL....love to hear from you.

The entry was followed by the submitter's name and e-mail address, as well as responses from a number of individuals who had information that helped this submitter with her query.

Magazine Queries
Just as you'll see queries about various families on message boards, genealogy magazines may also carry message sections where genealogists post questions about families they are researching. One of the most widely read genealogy magazines that posts queries is *Family History* magazine, published by Everton's Genealogical Helper (Everton's Family History Network, PO Box 368, Logan, Utah 84323-0368, Tel. 800/443-6325). Their query section is called Bureau of Missing Ancestors, and for a small fee you can post information about an ancestor for whom you are seeking information. You can subscribe to the magazine by writing to the above address, calling their toll-free number, or by visiting their website at **www.everton.com/shopper/**. At the time of this printing, the subscription price was under $30.00 for a 6-issue, one-year subscription.

Be a Detective!
Finding other family members or others working on your family line sometimes requires a great deal of creativity and curiosity. The more you have of these sleuth-like virtues, the more likely you are to be able to find someone who shares your interest in your family line. As you poke and prod in different and various places looking for your ancestors, keep on

the look out for names of others who are looking also, or who are working on the same lines as you.

I have been known to go to the (electronic) white pages that covered an area within a 50-mile radius of the locality where my ancestors lived and found individuals of the same surname. A short letter or even a phone call announcing my search has often paid big dividends. A bit impatient by nature, I am always anxious to get information quickly. With long distance phone rates running 5 to 7 cents a minute with major long distance carriers, a long distance phone call is often less expensive than a letter to contact possible cousins via phone. As a bonus, you get information immediately, and sometimes you meet the nicest people that way.

Internet message boards, magazine query ads, the **FamilySearch website** and other websites often contain the e-mail addresses as well as postal addresses of those working on a given line. These are invaluable assists in helping you to find others who are working on your line.

Is Anyone Out There? Checklist

____ Decide who you want to do research on.

____ Evaluate the various resources available for contacting others who are doing research on your family. (Internet message boards, magazine queries, genealogical societies, etc.)

____ Decide which is best for your available resources – do you have Internet access? Cost of magazine subscriptions and magazine queries, etc.

____ Be persistent!

____ Be willing to share what you have for individuals who place queries about the surnames you are researching.

17. PROFESSIONAL GENEALOGISTS

If you think you have hit a stone wall, that you simply don't have the money, time or skills to go a step further on a given family line, are you done? Do you have any options at all? Of course. While genealogy may be a hobby to you, it provides a living to thousands of individuals and organizations around the world. And these professional genealogists will be happy to help you move your line forward – for a price. But before you rush right out and secure the services of a professional genealogist, there are a few things you should consider. Fortunately for you, I have included those things on the next few pages, so read on.

Is Now The Time?
I thlnk you should ask yourself if now is the time to retain a professional genealogist. The detective work is the fun part for me, and the more elusive a given ancestor is, the more fun I have (okay – maybe I experience a *little* frustration!). Also, I have often found that if I cease looking so hard for someone and turn my attention to other family members – like the spouse, siblings, parents, etc., invariably I stumble across something about the elusive person that either solves the mystery for me, or takes me in a new direction where the mystery is eventually solved.

Do you remember taking those big tests periodically in school? You know the ones – the Iowa tests, or the California tests – the ones that were sponsored by the government? I remember my teachers and parents preparing me for the tests and telling me that if I hit a problem that I couldn't figure out, to leave it and complete the easier ones, then return to the ones that I was struggling with. Being an obedient child, I did that. Often, after just a few minutes away from the problem I would come back and see exactly how to do it.

So it has been time and again for me and elusive ancestors. I will often leave off researching for an individual when I hit a seeming dead end and focus on other individuals or even completely separate family lines. Returning after a period of time (often weeks or months later), I would see a clue that had escaped me prior to that. Following that new thread often yielded the results that had escaped me such a short time before.

Okay – It's Time

So let's assume that for whatever reason, you feel the time is right. Perhaps you really need to continue in your search for a given ancestor to prove your membership in a certain Native American tribe, or to link you to an ancestor who came to America on the Mayflower. Or perhaps the genealogy is being done as a present for someone. Where to start? First of all, since you will be paying for this service, decide exactly what it is you are looking for. Before you even contact a professional genealogist, know who you want to find, and how far you want the research to progress. Do you want one line followed, or several? If you provide the researcher with a really wide array of things sort of related to what you really want, you may pay a lot of money, end up with a lot of information, and still not have found the individual you were seeking in the first place. So – be very specific.

Next, gather all the information you have already gleaned on the individual or family line you want researched. No sense paying a researcher to do the work you have already done. One caution here, though: make sure the information you give the researcher is all correct! If it is not, then the researcher is likely to waste a lot of time (and a lot of your money!) looking in the wrong state, or for the wrong parents, or in the wrong decade! Provide copies of any documentation you have that provides verification of the information you are providing the researcher.

Also provide any dead-ends your research has run into, but make certain they really are dead ends. After you have done all that, it's time to decide on an individual researcher. Researchers advertise often in genealogy magazines, on the Internet and in the yellow pages. While you may choose any of them, I would suggest that your first stop ought to be to check with a professional genealogists' organization. There are several to choose from; here are the best:

The Board of Certification of Genealogists (BCG)

The BCG is a certification board with the following non-nonsense charter:

To foster public confidence in genealogy as a respected branch of history by promoting an attainable, uniform standard of competence and ethics among genealogical practitioners; and by publicly recognizing persons who meet that standard.

Genealogists seeking certification will be expected to pass several genealogy-related tests and submit project work in the area they are seeking to be certified. The BCG offers five levels of certification:

•Certified Genealogical Records Specialist (CGRS)
•Certified Lineage Specialist (CLS)
•Certified Genealogist (CG)
•Certified Genealogical Lecturer (CGL)
•Certified Genealogical Instructor (CGI)

Each classification requires specific testing and/or project work to qualify for certification. BCG offers to serve as an arbitrator for one of their certified genealogists should a disagreement arise between the genealogist and a client.

A list of certified genealogists is provided on their website or from the address listed below:

The Board of Certification of Genealogists
PO Box 14291
Washington, DC 20044
E-mail: office@bcgcertification.org
Website: www.bcgcertification.org

The International Commission for the Accreditation of Professional Genealogists (ICAPGEN)
The ICAPGEN is an organization that certifies professional genealogists according to a set of oral and written exams. Applicants are tested in both theoretical research methodologies as well as in the location and use of original documents unique to their regional areas. Research strategies, knowledge of available documents and their contents are all part of the ICAPGEN certification process. In addition to being able to pass a test, successful candidates must demonstrate at least 1,000 hours of research in the area for which they are seeking certification.

Certification areas include the following:

•Eastern United States
•Midwestern United States
•New England

•Southern United States
•Canada (British)
•Canada (French)
•American Indian
•LDS Church Records

The ICAPGEN organization has over 100 certified professional genealogists listed on their website that you may contact, or you may write to the
website below to get a list of certified genealogists.

International Commission for the Accreditation of
Professional Genealogists
PO Box 1144
Salt Lake City, Utah 84110-1144
Tel. 888/463-6842
E-mail: information@icapgen.org
Website: www.icapgen.org

The Association of Professional Genealogists (APG)
The APG is also dedicated to furthering the ethical practice of professional genealogy. While the first two organizations listed above are
certification boards, APG is an association for genealogists to join. Their
website includes some common sense information about engaging a
professional genealogist, including what you might expect to pay,
payment arrangements, dispute resolution, etc. (Should a dispute arise
between an APG-certified genealogist and a client, APG will serve as
arbitrator for the two parties.) The APG website features a searchable
database of certified genealogists. Just enter the specialty you are
seeking (geographic, ethnic, etc.), and you'll receive a list of those
genealogists certified in that area of genealogy.

The Association of Professional Genealogists (APG)
PO Box 745729
Arvada, Colorado 80006-5729
Tel. 303/422-9371
E-mail: admin@apgen.org
Website: www.apgen.org

Before you engage a professional genealogist, I'd recommend checking
out several first. Find out if they have experience in the specific area you
are interested in. If you are seeking help doing ethnic genealogy, find out
how much experience each genealogist has in ethnic research in

general, and their specific experience in the ethnic area you are interested in.

What Will It Cost?

Professional genealogists generally charge by the hour, and their rates are generally in the $25 to $75 per hour range. Some charge more, but they are generally specialists who work in highly specialized fields.

Financial arrangements are as varied as the people who enter into them. A popular and common way to engage a genealogist is to pay them a retainer to perform a certain amount of work. Once that work has been completed, then the client can decide whether he or she wants to continue with the genealogist's services. Consider setting a "not-to-exceed" price so that you have no nasty surprises.

Professional Genealogists Checklist

___ Decide whether you have gone as far your abilities and/or resources allow.

___ Decide what you can afford to pay a professional genealogist.

___ Go to any of the professional genealogical organizations to find a certified genealogist.

___ Locate a professional genealogist who has experience and skills in the area of the country or ethnicity that you want to have researched.

___ Share any information you have about the family you want to have researched with the genealogist. This will keep him or her from discovering research that you already have done.

___ Identify the specific information you want the genealogist to find.

___ Agree on a price (get it in writing!)

___ Consider a "not-to-exceed" price.

18. HELP YOUR DESCENDANTS!

Consider the following scenario: You are helping your grandmother clean out the attic of her old Victorian home, and while working you discover a dusty old book in one corner of the attic. Taking it into the light, you open it and discover that it is a personal history that your 2nd great grandfather had written near the end of his life. As you scan its pages, you realize that he provided detailed information about his life and its joys and challenges as well as his hopes and dreams. Included on its old yellowed pages you find information about his parents, his sweetheart and each of his children. As a bonus, he wrote about various and sundry items that were happening on the national scene: a presidential election (and who he favored and why), how the family was weathering an economic downturn, his views on various wars or conflicts the country was involved in, etc.

What a find! What a joy that would be for you! Now - have you considered that you have it within your power to provide that very same information to your own descendants? If you wrote a personal history or perhaps even kept a daily (or weekly or monthly) journal, it could be your genealogical gift to your posterity. With a little bit of effort on your part, such a document could preserve important genealogical information for your children, grandchildren and beyond. It could provide a peek into your soul if you share your feelings and thoughts about the life around you.

Writing a Personal History

I have to make a confession: I started writing a personal history at least a half dozen times before I finally found a formula that worked and allowed me to finish it. But like so many other things that are worthwhile, sometimes persistence is the greatest asset you can have to accomplish something - but a formula helps too.

After trying several different methods, I finally hit on a pretty simple and

HELP YOUR DESCENDANTS!

successful one. Following are the steps I followed to successfully complete my personal history:

- Write down a list of "chapters" that you would like to have in your personal history.
- Under each chapter heading, write a list of experiences or information that should be included in that chapter.
- Decide on a time during the week that you will write on a regular basis.
- Decide whether you want to include photographs in your history.
- Begin writing.
- Continue writing.
- Just do it!

Chapters

Begin your personal history by writing down a list of chapter headings. This will be the beginning of your personal history. If you are like me, the number of chapters will grow as you think of experiences that do not fit into an existing chapter; when that happens, just start another chapter heading. Don't just write the chapters down in a Table of Contents, but write them on separate pages of a pad of paper or separate them by page breaks if you are using a computer.

Next, spend a few minutes with each chapter and write down a list of everything you think should go into that chapter. Don't worry about having an exhaustive list to begin with - I can tell you from experience that as you write your history, additional memories will come to you. When that happens, pause in your writing and go to whichever chapter the experience you just remembered belongs in, and jot down a few lines - just enough to remember what it was about so you can write about it later. Then return to the chapter you were writing in.

Below is a list of chapters that eventually ended up in my personal history. It is certainly not an exhaustive list, but the one that applied to my life:

- Summary
- Genealogy
- Birth
- The early years
- Schooling years
- College
- Friends
- Marriage

- Children
- Employment
- Memorable vacations
- Significant people in my life
- Significant personal events
- Significant world events
- Dan on Dan (my thoughts about me)

You will doubtless have other chapters that I do not have: military service, living abroad, my political career, My Life as a Spy, etc.

Now take each chapter and list events you want to be sure and include in your history, like this:

- **Memorable vacations**
    - Disneyland
    - Camping at Mt. Shavano
    - Yellowstone
    - Sand dunes
    -- The beach in San Diego
    - DisneyWorld
    - Western Europe
    -- Ireland
    - Scotland
    - Etc.
- **Significant world events**
    - Man walking on the moon
    - Kennedy assassination
    - Nixon resignation
    - The Challenger explosion
    - The Gulf War
    - Clinton impeachment
    - Bush/Gore photo-finish presidential election
    - Terrorist attacks on the World Trade Center
    - Etc.

Again, the reason for this list is just to provide a memory jogger for when you begin your own writing. Don't worry about making it an exhaustive list - just write down what comes to mind now. I guarantee you that more ideas will come as you begin writing.

Set a Regular Time
Once you have written down your chapters and have a list of events to

write about under each chapter, it's time to set your writing schedule. Few individuals have the time or ability to sit down and write their personal history from beginning to end. Life happens to interrupt that plan for most of the people I know.

If possible, select a time that works best in your schedule. In my case, I decided to write every Sunday afternoon for a few hours. I decided to do it within an hour of returning from church services each Sunday. Some Sundays things came up and I was not able to write; but generally I was able to put in at least one or two hours each Sunday afternoon, occasionally more. Within a year, I had a completed personal history. Perhaps this time will work for you, or maybe it is an entirely different day of the week or time of the day. Perhaps you decide to write each day while your young ones are napping. Or perhaps you decide to load your personal history on your laptop and only write while you are sitting in your hotel room while you are traveling on business. That way, you don't take time away from your family, and you pass the time much more productively than if you watched whatever drivel you could find on the TV.

Regardless or the time or place you choose, the important thing is to set aside a day and time, or a situation (like while you are traveling) and then stick to it.

Additional Help
There are many helpful books on the market today that will guide you to look at your life and have a number of questions that will spark memories and help you begin writing your personal history. I have listed a few of the better ones at the end of this chapter in the Additional Resources section.

Keep a Journal
While writing a personal history is like writing the Reader's Digest version of your life, keeping a daily, weekly or monthly journal is more like writing the original text. I say a "daily, weekly or monthly journal" because it is my personal experience that with life's pace these days, it is very difficult to set aside time each day to keep a journal. But as with writing your personal history, I believe that if you set aside a set time each week, or perhaps each month (like the first Sunday of each month) to write in a journal, you will be more successful than if you try to write every day. If you also write entries for significant events - new jobs, the birth of your children, significant national events, etc. - then you will capture many important things that will be of interest to your children and others.

I have kept a journal for years, although I must admit, not as faithfully as I would like. But it has already borne wonderful fruit for our family. For example, when we celebrate each of our children's birthdays, they enjoy hearing my wife and I read what we wrote about them in our journals on the day of their birth. We wrote about what the day was like, the kind of birthing room, how long labor was, the doctor's name, and our feelings about each new child we welcomed into the world. (Even the teenagers like to hear these stories time and again.)

Each year on New Year's Day (or shortly therafter), I write a "State of the World" and "State of the Quillen Family" entry. It includes what is going on in the world and nation, who the president of the United States is (and my thoughts about that person), and those kinds of things. Then I write about our family - my employment situation, including my salary, what each of the family members is doing, and relatively mundane details about our life: the value of our home, our house payment, the cost of groceries (the price of a gallon of milk, a pound of hamburger, etc.) and the cost of gas. Already it is fun for me to look back and read about times in our early marriage. I am amazed at how nervous we were to step up to the $356 per-month house payment for our first home, for example. Imagine what my great grandchildren will think when they read those same words. And don't you wish you had a daily - or even weekly or monthly - journal of one of your ancestors from 100 years ago?

In a daily journal, I would suggest that you share your feelings and thoughts about things. Share your deep love for your sweetheart and your children, share your concerns, challenges and disappointments. Celebrate your successes and your joys. My wife is particularly good at writing her feelings in her journal. She will read mine from time to time, and complains that I have a tendency to just provide the facts of what happened, as opposed to the feelings. She says my journal is more like business writing. She is right, of course, and our descendants will learn different things about my wife and I when reading our journals 100 years from now. Of course, my dry, these-are-the-facts, Ma'am record tells them something about me too!

What Do I Do Now?
Okay – so you have taken my advice and written a personal history. Now what do you do with it? You can leave it on your computer and risk losing it in the next hard drive crash, but there is much more that you can do with it. After I finished mine, I made copies of it and gave it to each of my family members. Although I did not, you may want to bind your history into book form. It doesn't have to be professionally bound like a book - you could

HELP YOUR DESCENDANTS!

bind it with a spiral binding at a local copy store, or simply put it in a three-ring binder. That last way is particularly appealing, since you could add chapters or expand chapters as you get older. I wrote my first (finished!) personal history the year I turned 40. The title was: *W. Daniel Quillen - The First Forty Years*. Because I didn't bind it, I am preparing an addition to it that will allow me to change the title to *W. Daniel Quillen - The First Fifty Years*. If I had bound the first edition, I could just produce a new edition every so often after that - a second, third, fourth volume, that covered the next decade or two. I could incur extra expense and have each subsequent edition bound like a book. Your local copy center and bindery can let you know what your options are, and what the cost for each option is.

By the way, the method I am suggesting for writing your personal history would work very well for writing a biography of an aging relative. If they are not going to do it themselves, this would make a great formula for eliciting the information from them so that you could write it for them. And what a joy for you - and for them if each Sunday (for example) they expected your phone call or visit to flesh out each chapter of their personal history. What a treasure that will be for you and for your (and their) descendants! And how nice it would be to spend time with that aging relative who, after all, won't be around forever.

Help Your Descendants! Checklist
____ Decide whether you want to write your own personal history.

____ Begin the process by writing down the chapters you think best represent the major aspects of your life. Write each chapter name on a separate piece of paper.
____ Under each chapter heading, write a list of the events that should be covered in that chapter.

____ Determine a time that will work best in your schedule for you to write your personal history.

____ Begin writing!

____ Continue writing!

Additional Resources
Green, Bob, and Fulford, D. G., To Our Children's Children: Preserving Family Histories for Generations to Come, Doubleday Publishing. (March 1993)

Keel, Philipp, All About Me, Bantam Doubleday Dell Publications. (February 1998)

Kempthorne, Charley, For All Time: A Complete Guide to Writing Your Family History, Heinemann Publishing. (September 1996)

Marshall, Carl and Marshall, David, The Book of Myself: A Do-It-Yourself Autobiography in 201 Questions, Hyperion Publishing. (January 1997)

Marshall, David and Kate, The Book of Us: A Journal of Your Love Story in 150 Questions, Hyperion Publishing. (February 1999)

19. IN SUMMARY

You are about to embark on one of the most enjoyable journeys of your life:

the journey to discover what makes you who you are. If your experience is like mine, this will be the beginning of a life-long hobby that will bring you a great deal of satisfaction and introduce you to new friends and long-lost cousins. It may even take you to far-flung corners of the world, either via the Internet or in person, in search of your roots. Below are the high points to remember when it comes to doing genealogy:

• Start with what you know.

• Expand to find out what relatives know.

• Before doing too much research, decide on a system of organization (you'll be really glad you did!). In the beginning, it doesn't need to be elaborate or even electronic, but just organize your records in a manner that makes the most sense to you.

• Always be aware of variations in spelling for names. Don't get locked into only the way your line of the family spells your surname.

• Vital records include birth, death and marriage certificates. Obtaining them for the information they contain should be your goal as a researcher.

• Genealogical societies can be valuable resources for assisting you in your genealogical research.

• Many libraries have extensive genealogical collections that may provide information about your ancestors.

SECRETS OF TRACING YOUR ANCESTORS

•The Internet is one of the greatest aids to genealogical research ever. The click of a mouse may help you learn information that has eluded you for years in your genealogical research.

•The LDS Church is one of the foremost genealogical organizations in the world. They have amassed over 750 million names in databases, books and microfilm, all of which is accessible to researchers of any religion. They have a large central library in Salt Lake City, with over 3,700 branches all over the world. Records can be ordered and sent to any branch library (called Family History Centers).

•Census records provide a wealth of information about your ancestors. Remember, however, that they are secondary resources, but can help you identify when and where your ancestors lived on certain dates.

•Military records are an often over looked source of genealogical information.

•There are many resources available that are devoted to ethnic research for your ancestors. These may assist you in finding information about ancestors that have eluded you to this point in your research.

•Don't feel alone — more than likely there are many individuals who are doing research on at least part of your family line. And they are almost always very willing to share the information that they have.

•If you feel you have exhausted your time resources and research skills, you may want to employ the services of a professional genealogist.

•Writing a personal history and/or keeping a journal is a gift to your posterity.

Again — once you embark on this path to who you are and where you came from, you are in for a treat indeed. May it be all you hope it to be.

APPENDIX

GLOSSARY OF TERMS

Ancestors – your progenitors, those from whom you descend: parents, grandparents and on up the family tree.

Ancestral File – the LDS Church's file of more than 40 million names of individuals whose genealogical information has been recorded as families. It is accessible to all who have an interest in genealogy, regardless of religious persuasion.

Bulletin Boards – this is a place where individuals can post queries about ancestors. Others read and may (hopefully) respond to these queries, providing important genealogical information. Also called Message Boards.

Census – an enumeration of the population, usually conducted by the government. It may provide only a tabulation of numbers, but may often provide the names of everyone living in the household at the time of the census. Censuses can be rich sources of information for genealogists.

Database – a software program that contains information that can be searched against various categories. For example, you can query a database looking for all your ancestors who were born in North Carolina, then search the same database for all ancestors named Robert. The results of each search will be displayed.

Daughters of the American Revolution (DAR) – a well-known genealogical society for those who can prove a connection to an ancestor who fought in the Revolutionary War.

Dawes Rolls – a census of the Five Civilized Tribes living in the Oklahoma Indian Territory.

Descendants – those who descend from an individual – their children, grandchildren, etc. Each considers this person their ancestor.

E-mail – an electronic form of information exchange. Imagine a letter that can be received in a matter of moments from when it was sent to anyplace in the world. Its emergence has been a boon for genealogists.

Family Group Sheet - this is a document that groups a family together under their father. Included will be a man, his wife and all of their children, along with important information about each person, such as their birth, marriage and death dates and places. It is one of the main forms used in genealogy research.

Family History – this term is often used interchangeably with genealogy. It is also used to describe a narrative account of a family, typically going beyond mere statistics and usually including stories and anecdotes of the individual family members.

Family History Centers – local genealogy libraries staffed by volunteers of the LDS Church where genealogists can access the LDS Church's vast genealogical records. They are open to any genealogist, regardless of religious persuasion. Over 3,700 Family History Centers exist around the world.

Family History Library – a very large genealogical research library owned and operated by the LDS Church. Staffed by volunteers, it has an enormous amount of worldwide genealogical information that is available to anyone, regardless of religious affiliation.

Five Civilized Tribes – those tribes of Native Americans who were moved into the reservations in Oklahoma Indian Territory. They were members of the Cherokee, Choctaw, Chickasaw, Creek and Seminole tribes.

Gazetteer – a dictionary for places, which gives you information about places (state, county, country, etc.).

GEDCOM - a standard software format that most genealogy software uses as a standard. If you are using a genealogy program that uses GEDCOM, you will be able to share your information with others more easily. GEDCOM is an acronym for **GE**nealogical **D**ata **COM**munication.

APPENDIX

Genealogy – the number one hobby in the world. It is a fascinating, scintillating past-time that involves the search for one's ancestors.

Guion Miller Roll – a census of members of the Cherokee tribe who were descendants of the individuals who participated in the 1835/1836 Trail of Tears – the forced relocation of the Cherokee Nation.

Hit – in Internet terms, a *hit* is the successful search for a topic that matches the criteria you entered in your search engine.

Home page – this is the first web page of any website. It often serves as a table of contents for other pages that may be available on the website.

Internet Service Provider (ISP) – a company that provides access to the Internet for a fee.

Maternal - used to describe which line of the family tree you are referring to. Your maternal grandfather is your mother's father.

Message Boards - this is a place where individuals can post queries about ancestors. Others read and may (hopefully) respond to these queries. Also called Bulletin Boards.

Mouse – the little thingy you use to navigate around the computer screen.

Parish – an ecclesiastical or governmental unit where genealogical records were often kept.

Paternal - used to describe which line of the family tree you are referring to. Your paternal grandfather is your father's father.

Pedigree Chart - this is a chart the will show at a glance what your "family tree" looks like, by showing in graphic form who your parents, grandparents, great grandparents, etc., are. A limited amount of genealogical information is included. This is an important genealogical form.

Personal events – genealogical data entered into genealogy software programs; for example: birth, marriage and death dates.

Personal History – this is a narrative account of one's life and history. Going beyond the statistics, it includes stories, thoughts and feelings of the individual.

Primary Source - these are genealogy records created at the time of the event. A birth certificate that was completed at the time of a birth would be considered a primary source.

Queries – from a genealogical perspective, requests for information about a particular person or family. This might be on a message board, in a genealogical publication or via e-mail.

SASE – this is the acronym for a self-addressed, stamped envelope. When you request information or vital statistics from government agencies, they generally require an SASE (also called SSE sometimes). It is good practice to include this when asking for information from individuals also.

Search engine – a site on the Internet that allows you to search for items on the Internet. Once you enter a word or words in the search engine, it will scour the Internet, looking for websites that contain those words. Well-known search engines are Yahoo!, Google, Ask Jeeves and Lycos.

Secondary Source - genealogy records where information is provided much later than the event. A tombstone or death certificate would be considered a primary source for death information, but a secondary source for birth information, since it is likely that the birth information was provided many years after the person's birth occurred.

Society of Mayflower Descendants- a well-known genealogical society for those who can prove a connection to an ancestor who came to America on the Mayflower.

Soundex – a phonetic/numeric index for various US censuses. It combines the first letter of a surname with numbers for the next three consonants to form a Soundex entry. This is then used to locate individuals in the census (it's easier to use than it sounds!).

Shtetl – a Jewish community.

Traditions – those stories that circulate around the family about great grandfather's exploits in the gold fields of California, or war stories, or how grandma and grandpa met. Besides being interesting, these stories often provide genealogical clues that help you find information on your ancestors.

Vital Records - this term is generally used to refer to genealogical records such as birth, marriage and death information. They are also called Civil Registration or Vital Statistics.

Web browser – a software package that allows you to navigate around the Internet, and is a valuable tool for genealogists. Two well-known browsers are Internet Explorer and Netscape Navigator.

STATE LIBRARIES & ARCHIVES

Alabama
Alabama Public Library Service, Tel. 334/213-3900; Tel. 800/723-8459 (Within Alabama only); www.apls.state.al.us/

Alaska
Alaska State Archives, Tel. 907/465-2700; www.library.state.ak.us/

Alaska State Library, Tel. 907/465-2910

Arizona
Arizona State Library, Archives &, www.dlapr.lib.az.us/

Arkansas
Arkansas State Library, Tel. 501/682-1527; www.asl.lib.ar.us/

California
California State Library, www.library.ca.gov/

California State Archives, www.sos.ca.gov/

Colorado
Colorado State Library, Tel. 303/866-6900; www.cde.state.co.us/ index_library.htm

Colorado State Archives, www.colorado.gov/dpa/doit/archives/

Connecticut
Connecticut State Library and Archives, Tel. 860/757-6500; www.cslib.org/

Delaware
Delaware State Library, www.lib.de.us/

Delaware Public Archives, archives.delaware.gov/

Florida
Florida State Library and Archives, Tel. 850/245-6600; dlis.dos.state.fl.us/

Georgia
Georgia Department of Archives and History, www.gpls.public.lib.ga.us/

Hawaii
Hawaii State Library, www.hcc.hawaii.edu/hspls/

Hawaii State Archives, Tel. 808/586-0329; www.hawaii.gov/dags/archives

Idaho
Idaho State Library, Tel. 208/334-2150; www.lili.org/isl/

Idaho State Historical Society, www.idahohistory.net/library_archives.html

Illinois
Illinois Sate Library, Tel. 217/85-5600; www.cyberdriveillinois.com/library/isl/isl.html

Illinois State Archives, www.sos.state.il.us/departments/archives/serv_sta.html

Indiana
Indiana State Library and Archives, www.statelib.lib.in.us/

Iowa
Iowa State Library, www.silo.lib.ia.us/

State Historical Society of Iowa, www.iowahistory.org/archives/index.html

Kansas
Kansas State Library, Tel. 785/296-3296; Tel. 800/432-3919; skyways.lib.ks.us/kansas/

Kansas State Historical Society, www.kshs.org

Kentucky
Kentucky State Library, Tel. 502/564-8300; www.kdla.state.ky.us/

APPENDIX

Louisiana
Louisiana State Library, Tel. 225/342-4923; www.kdla.state.ky.us/

Louisiana State Archives, Tel. 225/922-1000; www.sec.state.la.us/archives/archives/archives-index.htm

Maine
Maine State Library, Tel. 207/287-5600; www.state.me.us/msl/index.html

Maine State Archives, Tel. 207/287-5795; www.state.me.us/sos/arc/

Maryland
Maryland State Library, Tel. 410/396-5430; www.pratt.lib.md.us/slrc/index.html

Maryland State Archives, Tel. 410/260-6400; www.mdarchives.state.md.us

Massachusetts
Massachusetts State Library, State House, Tel. 617/727-2590; Tel. 800/952-7403 (in state); www.state.ma.us/lib/

Massachusetts State Archives, www.state.ma.us/sec/arc/arcidx.htm

Michigan
Michigan State Library and Archives, Tel. 517/373-1580; www.libofmich.lib.mi.us/; www.sos.state.mi.us/history/archive/archive.html

Minnesota
Minnesota State Library, Tel. 681/582-8722; cfl.state.mn.us/library/

Minnesota State Historical Society, Tel. 651/296-6126; www.mnhs.org

Mississippi
Mississippi State Library, Tel. 800/647-7542; www.mlc.lib.ms.us/

Mississippi State Archives, Tel. 601/359-6850; *www.mdah.state.ms.us/*

Missouri
Missouri State Library, www.sos.state.mo.us/library/

Missouri State Archives, www.sos.state.mo.us/archives/

Montana
Montana State Library, Tel: 406/444-3115; msl.state.mt.us/

Montana Historical Society, Tel. 406/444-2694; www.his.state.mt.us/

Nebraska
Nebraska State Library, Tel. 402/471-2045; *www.nlc.state.ne.us/index.html*

Nebraska State Historical Society, www.nebraskahistory.org/

Nevada
Nevada State Library and Archives, Tel. 775/684-3360; dmla.clan.lib.nv.us/docs/nsla/archives/

New Hampshire
New Hampshire State Library, Tel. 603/271-2392; www.state.nh.us/nhsl/contact.html

New Hampshire State Archives, Tel. 603/271-2236; www.state.nh.us/state/index.html

New Jersey
New Jersey State Library and Archives, Tel. 609/292-6274Tel. 609/292-6274; www.njstatelib.org/

New Mexico
New Mexico State Library, Tel. 505/476-9700; www.stlib.state.nm.us/

New Mexico State Records Center and Archives, Tel. 505/476-9700 Tel. 505/476-9700; www.state.nm.us/cpr/

New York
New York State Library, Tel. 518/474-5355; unix2.nysed.gov/

New York State Archives and Records, www.archives.nysed.gov/aindex.shtml

North Carolina
North Carolina State Library,Tel. 919/733-3270; Tel. 919/733-3270; statelibrary.dcr.state.nc.us/

APPENDIX

North Carolina Division of Archives, Tel. 919/733-3952; www.ah.dcr.state.nc.us/sections/archives/arch/default.htm

North Dakota
North Dakota State Library, Tel. 701/328-2492; ndsl.lib.state.nd.us/

North Dakota State Archives, Tel. 701/328-2091Tel. 701/328-2091; www.state.nd.us/hist//sal.htm

Ohio
Ohio State Library, Tel. 614/644-7061Tel. 614/644-7061; winslo.state.oh.us/

Ohio State Archives, www.ohiohistory.org/resource/statearc/

Oklahoma
Oklahoma State Library, www.odl.state.ok.us/index.html

Oklahoma State Archives, www.odl.state.ok.us/oar/

Oregon
Oregon State Library, Tel. 503/378-4243; www.osl.state.or.us/home/admin/stlib_info.html

Oregon State Archives, Tel. 503/373-070; arcweb.sos.state.or.us/banners/contactus.htm

Pennsylvania
Pennsylvania State Library, Tel. 717/783-5950; www.statelibrary.state.pa.us/libraries/site/default.asp

Pennsylvania State Archives, Tel. 717/783-3281; www.phmc.state.pa.us/bah/dam/overview.htm

Rhode Island
Rhode Island State Library, www.olis.state.ri.us/

Rhode Island State Archives, Tel. 401/222-2353; www.state.ri.us/archives/

Rhode Island Historical Society,Tel. 401/331-8575; www.rihs.org

South Carolina, Tel. 803/734-8666; www.state.sc.us/scsl/

South Carolina Archives and History Center, Tel. 803/896-6100; www.state.sc.us/scdah/

South Dakota
South Dakota State Library, Tel. 605/773-3131; www.sdstatelibrary.com/

South Dakota State Historical Society, Tel. 605/773-3458; www.sdhistory.org/

Tennessee
Tennessee State Library and Archives, Tel. 615/741-2764; www.state.tn.us/sos/statelib/

Texas
Texas State Library and Archives, Tel. 512/463-5480; www.tsl.state.tx.us/

Utah
Utah State Library, library.utah.gov/

Utah State Archives, Tel. 801/538-3012; www.archives.state.ut.us

Vermont
Vermont State Library, Tel. 802/828-3261; dol.state.vt.us/

Vermont State Archives, vermont-archives.org/

Virginia
Virginia State Library and Archives, Tel. 804/692-3500; www.lva.lib.va.us/

Washington
Washington State Library, Tel. 360/704-5200; www.statelib.wa.gov/

Washington State Archives, Tel. 360/902-4151; www.secstate.wa.gov/ archives/search.aspx

Washington DC
The Library of Congress, 202/707-5000; www.loc.gov/

West Virginia
West Virginia State Library, Tel. 304/558-2041; www.wvlc.lib.wv.us/ html/verticalnavigation/reflibrary.html

West Virginia State Archives, www.wvculture.org/history/genealog.html

Wisconsin
Wisconsin Division of Libraries, www.dpi.state.wi.us/dpi/dlcl/index.html

Wisconsin State Historical Society, www.wisconsinhistory.org/index.html

Wyoming
Wyoming State Library, Tel. 307/777-7283; www-wsl.state.wy.us/

Wyoming State Archives, Tel. 307/777-7826; wyoarchives.state.wy.us/
index.html

STATE DEPARTMENTS OF VITAL STATISTICS

Following are the mailing addresses of each state's Department of Vital Records. Also included are the rates for birth and death certificates. Address your request to the (State Name) Department of Vital Records. Note that many states are now charging additional fees – some of them nothing short of exorbitant – if you want to order either over the phone or on the internet using your credit card (one state charges $46 to use your credit card!). So, you'll have to weigh the value of getting the certificates a little sooner vs. waiting a few more days.

Most of the states listed here have unfortunately caught on to the popularity of genealogy and the resultant revenues that can be gleaned from charges for certificates. Since the last edition of this book, certificate costs have risen in almost every state, some of them doubling or even tripling! Still, most are within a price range that most individuals would consider reasonable.

Many states charge a non-refundable search fee, generally equal to the cost of the certificate. The search fee usually includes the cost of the first copy of the certificate found.

Alabama
Birth: $12.00, Death: $12.00
Tel. 334/206-5418; www.alapubhealth.org/vital

Alaska
Birth: $10.00, Death: $10.00

Tel. 907/465-3392; www.hss.state.ak.us/dph/dph_home.htm

Arizona
Birth: $10.00 - $15.00, Death: $10.00
Tel. 602/255-3260; vitalrec.com/az.html

Arkansas
Birth: $12.00, Death: $8.00
Tel. 501/661-2134; www.healthyarkansas.com/certificates/
certificates.html#Death

California
Birth: $13.00, Death: $15.00
Tel. 916/445-2684; www.dhs.ca.gov/chs/OVR/OrderCert.htm

Colorado
Birth: $15.00 Death: $15.00
Tel. 303/692-2200; www.cdphe.state.co.us

Connecticut
Birth: $5.00 Death: $5.00
Tel. 860/509-7897; www.dph.state.ct.us/OPPE/hpvital.htm

Delaware
Birth: $10.00, Death: $10.00
Tel. 302/739-4721; www.state.de.us

Florida
Birth: $9.00, Death: $5.00
Tel. 904/359-6930; www.doh.state.fl.us/planning_eval/vital_statistics/
index.html

Georgia
Birth: $10.00, Death: $10.00
Tel. 404/656-4750; www.ph.dhr.state.ga.us

Hawaii
Birth: $10.00, Death: $10.00
Tel. 808/586-4533; www.hawaii.gov/doh/records

Idaho
Birth: $13.00, Death: $13.00
Tel. 208/334-5988; www.state.id.us/dhw

APPENDIX

Illinois
Birth: $15.00, Death: $10.00
Tel. 217/782-6554; www.idph.state.il.us

Indiana
Birth: $10.00, Death: $8.00
Tel. 317/233-2700; www.vitalrec.com/in.html

Iowa
Birth: $15.00, Death: $15.00
Tel. 515/281-4944; http://www.idph.state.ia.us/eh/health_statistics.asp

Kansas
Birth: $12.00, Death: $13.00
Tel. 785/296-1400; www.kdhe.state.ks.us/vital

Kentucky
Birth: $10.00, Death: $6.00
Tel. 502/564-4212; chfs.ky.gov/dph/vital/

Louisiana
Tel. 504/568-5152; www.oph.dhh.louisiana.gov/recordsstatistics/
vitalrecords/docs/packet13%20%2010%2003.doc

Maine
Birth: $15.00, Death: $15.00
Tel. 207/287-3184; www.cdc.gov/nchs/howto/w2w/maine.htm

Maryland
Birth: $12.00, Death: $12.00
Tel. 410/764-3038; mdpublichealth.org/vsa/html/apps.html

Massachusetts
Birth: $18.00, Death: $18.00
Tel. 785/296-1400; www.mass.gov/dph/bhsre/rvr/rvr.htm

Michigan
Birth: $15.00, Death: $15.00
Tel. 517/335-8666; www.michigan.gov/mdch/0,1607,7-132-
4645_4702—,00.html

Minnesota
Birth: $13.00, Death: $10.00

Tel. 612/676-5129; www.health.state.mn.us/divs/chs/osr/index.html

Mississippi
Birth: $12.00, Death: $10.00
Tel. 601/576-7981; www.msdh.state.ms.us/msdhsite/_static/
31,0,109.html

Missouri
Birth: $15.00, Death: $13.00
Tel. 573/751-6400; www.health.state.mo.us/BirthAndDeathRecords/

Montana
Birth: $12.00, Death: $12.00
Tel. 406/444-2685; vhsp.dphhs.mt.gov/dph_l2.htm

Nebraska
Birth: $8.00, Death: $8.00
Tel. 402/471-2871; www.hhs.state.ne.us

Nevada
Birth: $13.00, Death: $10.00
Tel. 800/992-0900; health2k.state.nv.us/forms/formindex.htm

New Hampshire
Birth: $15.00, Death: $15.00
Tel. 603/271-4650; www.state.nh.us

New Jersey
Birth: $10.00, Death: $10.00
Tel. 609/292-4087; www.state.nj.us/health/vital/vital.shtml

New Mexico
Birth: $10.00, Death: $10.00
Tel. 505/827-0121; www.health.state.nm.us

New York
Birth: $30.00, Death: $30.00
Tel. 518/474-3077; www.health.state.ny.us

North Carolina
Birth: $15.00, Death: $15.00
Tel. 919/733-3526; vitalrecords.dhhs.state.nc.us/vr/index.html

APPENDIX

North Dakota
Birth: $7.00, Death: $5.00
Tel. 701/328-2360; www.vitalnd.com/

Ohio
Birth: $15.00, Death: $15.00
Tel. 614/466-2531; www.odh.state.oh.us/

Oklahoma
Birth: $10.00, Death: $10.00
Tel. 405/271-4040; www.health.state.ok.us/program/vital

Oregon
Birth: $20.00, Death: $20.00
Tel. 503/731-4095; egov.oregon.gov/DHS/ph/chs/order/faqs.shtml#rec-cost

Pennsylvania
Birth: $9.00, Death: $9.00
Tel. 724/656-3100; www.dsf.health.state.pa.us/health/cwp/
view.asp?a=168&Q=229939&healthRNavrad2F756=I#

Rhode Island
Birth: $15.00, Death: $15.00
Tel. 401/222-2811; www.health.state.ri.us

South Carolina
Birth: $12.00, Death: $12.00
Tel. 803/898-3432; www.scdhec.net/vr/

South Dakota
Birth: $10.00, Death: $10.00
Tel. 605/773-4961; www.state.sd.us/doh/VitalRec/index.htm

Tennessee
Birth: $12.00, Death: $7.00
Tel. 615/741-1763; www2.state.tn.us/health/vr/

Texas
Birth: $11.00, Death: $9.00
Tel. 512/458-7111; www.tdh.state.tx.us/bvs

Utah
Birth: $18.00, Death: $3.00
Tel. 801/536-6105; health.utah.gov/vitalrecords/

Vermont
Birth: $9.50, Death: $9.50
Tel. 802/863-7275; www.healthyvermonters.info/hs/vital/obtain.shtml

Virginia
Birth: $12.00, Death: $12.00
Tel. 804/662-6200; www.vdh.state.va.us/vitalrec/

Washington
Birth: $17.00, Death: $17.00
Tel. 360/236-4300; www.doh.wa.gov/EHSPHL/CHS/cert.htm

Washington D.C.
Birth: $12.00 (short), $18.00 (long), Death: $12.00
Tel. 202/783-1809; www.ci.washington.dc.us/health

West Virginia
Birth: $5.00, Death: $5.00
Tel. (304) 558-2931; www.wvdhhr.org/bph/oehp/hsc/vr/birtcert.htm

Wisconsin
Birth: $12.00, Death: $7.00
Tel. 608/266-1371; www.dhfs.state.wi.us/VitalRecords

Wyoming
Birth: $12.00, Death: $12.00
Tel. 307/777-7591; wdhfs.state.wy.us/vital_records

INDEX

Genealogy Notes

Genealogy Notes

Genealogy Notes

❀